The Gospel of John

New Metaphysical Version

Translator: *Bil Holton, Ph.D., LUT*

Editor: *Cher Holton, Ph.D., LUT*

Prosperity Publishing House

The Gospel of John
New Metaphysical Version
©2010 Prosperity Publishing House
All Rights Reserved

The *New Metaphysical Version* text may be quoted and/or reprinted in any form [written, visual, electronic, or audio] up to and inclusive of one hundred twenty five [125] words without the express written permission of the publisher, providing notice of copyright appears on the title or copyright page of the work as follows:

> *The Scriptural quotations contained herein are from the*
> *Gospel of John, New Metaphysical Version.*
> *Copyright 2010 by Prosperity Publishing House.*
> *Used by permission. All rights reserved.*

When quotations from the NMV [New Metaphysical Version] are used in non-saleable media, such as church bulletins, transparencies, meditation/prayer readings, etc., a copyright notice is not required, but the initials NMV must appear at the end of each quotation.

Quotations and/or reprints in excess of one hundred twenty-five [125] words, as well as other permission requests, including commercial use, must be approved in writing by *The Gospel of John, NMV,* Permissions Office, Prosperity Publishing House, 1405 Autumn Ridge Drive, Durham, NC 27712.

ISBN: 978-1-893095-62-5

Library of Congress Control Number: 2009914060

Through the quantum filter of the Cosmic Christ, physicality [all things] is possible. It is only through the instrumentality of the Christ Presence that potential morphs into form. This is possible because consciousness is the ground of all being.
[John 1:3]

Acknowledgments

I offer my heartfelt gratitude and love to my wonderful wife and soulmate, Cher, for her faith, support, love, and incredible editing, layout, and proofing as she stood by me throughout this entire project.

I also gratefully acknowledge the love, commitment, and clerical expertise of Nancy Eubanks, who assisted in the creation of this New Metaphysical Version of John through her tireless typing, enthusiastic support, and personal insights.

Table of Contents

Acknowledgments iii
To Students of Truth xi

Chapter One
The Word Becomes Flesh 1
Our John the Baptizer Provisional Awareness 2
The Baptizer Affidavit 3
The Spotless Lamb of God 5
Inaugurating Our Spiritual Powers 6

Chapter 2
The Wedding in Cana 9
Our Predictable Chemicalization 11
Upgrading Our Consciousness 12

Chapter Three
Nicodemusian Obstetics 13
The Only Way to Eternal Life 15
The Presence of the Indwelling Cosmic Christ 15
Bridling the Intellect 16
Christship Through Karmic Matriculation 17

Chapter Four
A Samaritan Moment 18
Spiritual Soil 21
Capitalizing on a Samaritan Moment 22
Bookmarking Our Faith With Action 23

Chapter Five
Our Anemic Bethesdaic Awkwardness 24
Our Eternal Heirship Recognized 26
Spiritual Attunement or Atrophy 29

Chapter Six
Transforming the Five Senses (Feeding the 5000) 31
Walking on Water 32
The Bread of Life 33
Moving From Sense Appetites to Spiritual Aspirations 38

Chapter Seven
The Undertone of Unbelief 39
Removing Error From Our Consciousness 40
The Limitations of a 'Skin School' Perspective 42
Handcuffed By a Warped Religiosity 43
The Cleansing Power of Christed Thought Currents 44
Sorting Out Our Divine Genogram 45

Chapter Eight
The Hypocrisy Associated With Unspiritualized Thoughts 46
A Theological 'San Andreas Fault' 48
Orphaning Ourselves From Our Divinity 49
Thwarting the Expression of Our Christ Potential 50

Chapter Nine
Horizontally Slanted and Vertically Challenged 54

Chapter Ten
We Are Shepherded by Our I Am Connection 59
Christed Actions Come From a Christed Consciousness 62

Chapter Eleven
Our Lazarus Legacy 65
The Gyrations of a Materially-Fixated Consciousness 70

Chapter Twelve
Our Love For the Truth Bathes Us in Understanding 72
The Urge to Resist Recharging Our Spiritual Batteries 74
Our Blossoming Christ Potential 74
From Mind Auction to Mind Action 75
Realizing Our Christ Potential or Rationing It 76
Pre-Christed Snapshot 78
The Omnipresent Ground of Being 79

Chapter Thirteen
When Our Consciousness is Bathed in Spiritual Understanding 80
Truncating Our Spiritual Growth 82
Our Newly Acquired Monistic Awareness 84

Chapter Fourteen
    The Way, the Truth, and the Life *85*
    The Powerful Omniactivity of the Holy Spirit *88*

Chapter Fifteen
    Our Christ Self, the True Vine *90*
    It Doesn't Make Sense to Deny Our Innate Divinity *93*

Chapter Sixteen
    Our Sense-corrupted Thoughts and Beliefs Must Go *94*
    The Holy Spirit's Sushumnic Effect *95*
    Less Lag Time More Real Time *96*
    No More Need For Involution or Evolution *97*

Chapter Seventeen
    We Must See Jesus as the Perfect Example,
      Not the Great Exception *99*
    Enfiring Our Thoughts, Words, and Actions *100*
    We Are Christed at Our Core *102*

Chapter Eighteen
    The Acoustics of Betrayal *103*
    A Treacherous Sense-Entranced Ego *104*
    We Must Prime Our Unprimed Faith *105*
    The Harshness of a Dogmatic Perspective *105*
    Denying Our Christ Connection *106*
    Choosing to Align or Rebel Against Our Christ Nature *107*

Chapter Nineteen
    When Our Egocentric World View Twists the Truth *109*
    Crossing Out Error in All Three Planes of Consciousness *111*
    Mastering Our Incarnational 'Calling' *112*
    The Quiet Roar of Enlightenment *114*

Chapter Twenty
    The Theodynamics of Our Resurrection Potential *115*
    Our Devotion to the Truth Electrifies Us *117*
    Over-Coming the Staining Effects of Error *118*
    Turning a Petulant Intellect Into Cosmic Intelligence *119*

Chapter Twenty-One
Achieving Complete Harmony With the
  Trinity of Trinities *121*
Out-Growing an Immature Faith and In-Growing
  a Full Throttle One *123*
The Quantum Legacy of Our Incarnational 'Stories' *124*

About the Translator *127*
Ordering Information *129*

To Students of Truth

The Bible, which is the story of humankind's evolution in consciousness, lends itself to four different levels of understanding:

1. literal [historical],
2. moral [sentimental],
3. allegorical/esoteric [intellectual], and
4. metaphysical [spiritual/ontological].

Given that perspective, I believe the awesome richness of New Testament Scripture should be genuinely explored in accordance with each level of understanding, with the proviso that the *fruits* of each understanding are consistent with the teachings of the Christ as Jesus.

Those who read or study Scripture only at the surface levels [literal and moral] may miss the deeper truths associated with the teachings. Unfortunately, a sober look at the effect these two levels of understanding have had on human history uncovers their inability to contribute significantly to creating heaven on earth. These two basic understandings of Scripture generally lend themselves to a condemnation of other faith traditions, and tend to be quite exclusive and judgmental in their dogmatic religious practice.

An intellectual understanding of Scripture can tend to remain a cognitive exercise with little movement toward the wisdom of the heart. Such a perspective may limit its views to the letter of the law and can be judgmental and fairly rigid in its interpretation.

A metaphysical/ontological understanding of Scripture takes *Bible* students into the realms of the spiritual and mystical. My aim is to give truth students a metaphysical view that stimulates their thinking and appreciation for the deeper meanings of Scripture. This metaphysical treatment is not meant to be the definitive metaphysical version of *The Gospel of John*. Hopefully, it will inspire other metaphysicians to add their wisdom and expertise to the growing body of metaphysical literature.

Sources:

The sources of metaphysical symbology used to render this unique version of *The Gospel of John* came from extraordinarily varied perspectives and time periods. It is with deep appreciation that this NMV was able to use insights from the following giants in metaphysical thought: Philo Judaeus, Origen, Pelagius, Zeno, Plato, Augustine, Hypatia, Dionysius, John Scotus Erigene, Meister Eckehart, George Fox, George Wilhem, St. Teresa of Avila, Friedrich Hegel, Emerson, Theodore Parker, Mary Baker Eddy, Emma Curtis

Hopkins, Nona Brooks, Paul Tillich, Charles Fillmore, Eric Butterworth, Teilhard de Chardin, Malinda Cramer, Emmet Fox, John Murray, Ella Wheeler Wilcox, Annie Rix, Thomas Troward, Ernest Wilson, Elizabeth Sand Turner, Warren Felt Evans, Ernest Holmes, Georgiana Tree West, Alice Bailey, Phineas Quimby, Geoffrey Hodson, Helena Blavatsky, Horatio Dresser, Alvin Kuhn, Rufus Collins Douglas, Edgar Cayce, and Dr. Paul Hasselbeck.

The Biblical Versions used as reference material for the NMV [New Metaphysical Version] in order to obtain the broadest possible band width of interpretation were: *The New Revised Standard Version, The NIV Rainbow Study Bible Version, the Authorized King James Version, George M. Lamsa's Translation from the Aramaic of the Pashitta, The Oxford Annotated Bible RSV, New International Version, the New Testament in Today's English Version, New American Standard Bible Version, Contemporary English Version, 21st Century King James Version, Worldwide English New Testament*, and the *Wycliffe New Testament*.

How to Use This Book:

This new version is intended for use along-side traditional versions, many of which are listed above. I recommend using this book as a study guide for congregational services, as well as for private study, meditation, and daily inspiration. It is suggested that traditional versions of the *Gospel of John* be used as supplements to this version, so that readers can compare traditional interpretations to the metaphysical content of this NMV verse-by-verse, chapter-by-chapter. I have provided both wings and landing gears with this metaphysical rendering, so that it is both practical and down to earth. In reading, you will see direct interpretation of key words identified within brackets [], while my editorial comments are in parentheses(). As you study, it is helpful to have these guides; when you read purely for spiritual enrichment or as a part of a service, you may want to omit the comments within the brackets and parentheses.

Final Comments:

I believe it has been to the detriment of all Christian history (as evidenced by the last 2,000 years of religious separatism, inquisitions, and wars) that religious leaders almost with one accord have belittled and condemned the importance and significance of a metaphysical perspective. Thankfully, a growing number of Truth students and higher consciousness practitioners today have opted for spiritual growth instead of religious myopia, and recognize that religion's failure to cultivate a healthy respect for a metaphysical approach to Scripture has been both unfortunate and costly. It is not an exaggeration to say this hesitation to explore higher truths has caused a pathological tear in the fabric of Christianity.

It is my sincere hope that you, the reader, will embrace the hidden wisdom contained in this uniquely metaphysical treatment of *The Gospel of John*. I believe you will be enriched beyond measure by the depth of its teachings and by the practical nature of its transcendental approach.

Chapter One

The Word Becomes Flesh

1. Before there was a physical universe [In the beginning[a]] there was the Cosmic Christ[b] [the Word], which is the ideational power [was with] of the One Reality [God, (Eternal Isness, the Absolute, the Infinite Invisibleness)]; and the Cosmic Christ [the Word] is God expressing Its Godness as the Cosmic Christ [the Word]. 2. The Cosmic Christ was *indivisibly* one with the One Reality (Eternal Isness, [God]) before matter itself came into existence.

3. Through the quantum filter of the Cosmic Christ, physicality [all things] is possible. It is only through the instrumentality of the Christ Presence that potential morphs into form. This is possible because consciousness is the ground of all being. 4. As a result of the Christ Presence there is eternality [life], and that eternality [life] is the existence [light] of the Christ in all things including humankind [man]. 5. This omnipresent Christ Presence [the light] underwrites [shines] all beingness, including human beingness which is generally unaware [darkness[c]] of its innate divinity.

6. Eventually we come to a place of expanded awareness, where we receive a highly transformative insight [man from God] which springs from a well-developed intellectual perception of Truth [our John quality]. 7. Intuitively, we realize this insight [witness] comes from Something [the Omnipresent Light] deep inside us. So touched are we by its purity and transcendentalness that we ready ourselves to transform all of our thoughts and inclinations [all men] into their higher spiritual essences. 8. Our illumined intellect [our John quality] is not the Christ [the Omnipresent Light],

---
[a] *From a monistic metaphysical perspective it is more aptly interpreted 'In a beginning' or 'In another beginning.' Quantum physics also suggests this cosmological viewpoint.*
[b] *The Cosmic Christ and Christ are synonymous and will be considered as such throughout this manuscript.*
[c] *Darkness represents our unawareness of, or the abject denial of, our innate divinity as spiritual beings in human form.*

it is only a Christed capacity [a witness] which springs from the Inner Light (the Christ Light). ⁹·The Cosmic Christ [the True Light] becomes enfleshed [came into the world].

¹⁰·Although the transcendent Cosmic Christ descends into sense consciousness [the world, the material universe], It is repressed by sense consciousness [the world], which fixates itself onto physical form [does not recognize its divine origin]. ¹¹·Because of the highly spiritualized quantum nature of the Cosmic Christ, Its *indivisibleness* with physical forms goes unnoticed by a sense-veneered human consciousness. Essentially, It (the Cosmic Christ) is veiled divinity. ¹²·However, a consciousness which is attuned to its divine nature [receives Him] becomes consciously one with the nature of its divine origin [believes in His name] and is able to produce divinely inspired ideas [children]. ¹³·It is important to know that divine ideas [children] do not come from the human personality [blood, flesh, (natural descent)], but from the Kingdom of God (Christ Consciousness) within us.

¹⁴·The Cosmic Christ [the Word] descends into matter [becomes enfleshed] and enfolds Itself into physicality [dwells among us]. The more enlightened we become, the more we realize our *indivisibleness* [glory] with the Christ expressing at the point of us. The enlightened us knows that the Cosmic Christ is the Only Begotten Son of God [the Father], which has become manifest as us to underwrite our return home [unification with the Eternal Isness]. This conscious unification will help us move beyond our attachments to the material universe [redeem us through grace], so we can live, move, and have our being in at-one-ment with the Absolute [Truth].

Our John the Baptizer Provisional Awareness

¹⁵·Our intellectual perception of Truth [our John the Baptizer quality] is a necessary pre-

requisite [a testimony] for the expanding awareness of our divine origin. In our illumined awareness – the Jesus of us – [he who comes after me], we understand that we are embodied Christs. It is this Perennial Quality [that which comes before me] which underwrites our very existence [he who has surpassed me]. ¹⁶·It is from Its timeless perfection [fullness] that we receive perennial pardons[d] [grace after grace] on our journey into the Light. ¹⁷·An illumined approach to our divinity requires that we intentionally draw ourselves out of error consciousness [symbolized by our Mosesic awareness] by denying false inclinations that keep us unaware of our True Self [laying down the law]. In other words, if we are not careful we may develop rickets of the soul. On the other hand, we must affirm our *indivisibleness* with the Christ as us so we are able to receive the full pardon [grace] that comes to those who fully understand and demonstrate their divine potential [manifest their Jesus Christ Nature]. ¹⁸·No unenlightened human personality can comprehend [see] its innate divinity. Only the Cosmic Christ (God expressed as the Only Begotten Son), which is the Ideational Form (Quantum Aspect) of the Eternal Isness [is close to the Father's heart] can make the relationship between Spirit and matter comprehensible.

The Baptizer Affidavit

¹⁹·Once we have a strong intellectual perception of the Truth [our mature John the Baptizer quality], we are able to eliminate the confusion and doubts which spring from religious biases [our Jewishness] and encrusted religious dogmas and beliefs [our Levitical and priestly natures]. ²⁰·It is clear from an enlightened intellectual perspective that our human personality is a facade,

---

[d] *Pardons refer to incarnation after incarnation; Christed thought after Christed thought which erases error thoughts; Christed choices after Christed choices which create Christed actions after Christed actions.*

a mask, a cosmetic cover-up. It is not who we really are. We eventually realize that our intellect is only a soul song in our Christogenesis. [21.] At this stage in our unfoldment (Christology) we do not comprehend, or have little comprehension of, our oneness with God [the Elijah of us] or the potentialized Jesus Christ aspect [the Prophet] of our Christology. [22.] Our human personality, driven by an unenlightened ego, is not able to grasp the truth that we are quantum expressions of the Christ in human form.

[23.] It takes a high degree of spiritual understanding [our Isaiahic capacity] to comprehend the formative power [voice] of the Christ which is enfleshed in human sense consciousness [the wilderness/desert]. It is our responsibility to prepare ourselves spiritually [make straight], so we can make the cosmic connections it takes to attain Christ Consciousness [the way of the Lord].

[24.] As we unfold spiritually, thoughts will spring from our dogmatic churchiness [our pharisaical bents] [25] which questions our authority to cleanse our consciousness of error [baptism]. Churchiness is sterile religiosity. It cannot lead us to the full demonstration of our innate divinity [our enfleshed Christedness], our eternal genealogy [our Elijahic capacity], or our fully potentialized Jesus Christ nature [the Prophet].

[26.] These truths reveal an extremely important spiritual dynamic. Our illumined intellect [our John the Baptizer quality] is only capable of cleansing [baptising] error thoughts out of our current consciousness. However, because we are Christ bearers we shall reach the level of adeptship in which we will fully demonstrate our divine potential [the unfamiliar One]. [27.] Indeed, as we transform our thinking, we will honor the Christ as Jesus Individuality [the one who comes after me], which is mightier than our human personality. Until we 'see the light,' we will not comprehend or appreciate our innate divinity or be able to unravel hidden truths with our limited egocentric understanding [our unworthiness to untie the thongs of His sandals].

[28.] It is only from a heightened spiritual perspective that we can cleanse [baptize] our consciousness of error and demonstrate our power over human limitations [Bethany], by bathing our consciousness in a stream [Jordan] of Christed thoughts instead of egocentric cravings.

The Spotless Lamb of God

[29.] When we reach a high level of spiritual awareness [the next day], our enlightened intellect [our John the Baptizer capacity] recognizes that in order to fully demonstrate our Christ potential [the Jesus of us], we must seek to live an unblemished life [the Lamb of God] characterized by the erasure of all errors [sins] from our consciousness [the world]. [30.] This fully demonstrated Christ potential [the adept Jesus of us] is superior [has surpassed me] to our illumined intellect, because It is the all-pervading Presence of the Absolute (the Eternal Isness, God, the Infinite Invisibleness, the Absolute). [31.] Although our intellect cannot fully comprehend our Christ potential [did not know Him], it is able to censor or neutralize discordant thoughts and inclinations [baptize with water] so we can raise our spiritual azimuths [might be revealed to Israel] to a more Christed level of awareness.

[32.] Working from our illumined intellect [our John the Baptizer quality], we can avoid giving power to outer appearances by rising above old error patterns and finding inner peace [the dove]. [33.] Make no mistake about it, an illumined intellect has an important role to play in our Christology. Although, as mentioned before, we cannot fully comprehend the Absolute [I myself did not know Him] even with an illumined intellect, we can be aware that a conscientious erasure of inharmonious thoughts and tendencies [water baptism] prepares our conscious mind to *field* the inflow of spiritual energies [Spirit descending]. This intellectual triage helps transform our thinking so we can become more fully aware of our innate divinity [be baptized by the Holy Spirit]. ³⁴· Intuitively we know that this mysterious veiled Presence is the Cosmic Christ [the Only Begotten Son of God].

Inaugurating Our Spiritual Powers

³⁵· As we elevate our spiritual awareness [the next day], our illumined intellect [our John the Baptizer quality] transforms sense thoughts into spiritual insights [two disciples]. ³⁶· These higher insights demonstrate our recognition that we can actualize our Christ potential [the Jesus of us] by seeking the Unblemished Life [become the Lamb of God].

³⁷· As we focus on elevating our human thoughts to their higher spiritual essences [the two disciples], we move closer [they follow Him] to realizing our Christ potential [the Jesus of us]. ³⁸· But the process demands empassioned clarity and discernment. For example, if we expect to fully demonstrate our Christ potential, our Guiding Life Principle [Rabbi/Teacher] must be that God (the One Reality, the Absolute) is the inviolate Source of our greater good. That insight is central to our unfoldment. We must never doubt the origin of our omniscient wisdom, omnipresent supply, omnipotent divinity, and omniactive vitality ["Where are you staying?"].

³⁹· Spirit constantly invites us to become consciously one with our Christ Self so that we can fully unfold [spend the day] into our perfection and wholeness.

40. As our Truth seeking intellect [our John the Baptizer quality] becomes more enlightened, we gain the inner strength [our Andrewness] which comes from our realized Christ potential [the Jesus of us]. 41. Our inner strength, coupled with the belief that we can turn hope into substance and possibility into probability [our Simon quality], helps us comprehend our evolving Christship [Messiahship]. 42. When our inner resolve is strong enough, it quickens our belief in manifesting our good [brings him to Jesus], which strengthens our faith [our Cephas (stone) foundation].

43. With this new understanding [the next day], our spiritual unfoldment [the Jesus of us] settles (rays forth) into our subconscious [Galilee] and begins to transform ["Follow Me."] and redirect [our Phillipness] subconscious error patterns, lifting them to their higher spiritual essences.

44. This energetic boost [the Phillip of us], fortified by our inner strength [our Andrew quality] and evolving faith [our Cephas/Peter quality], becomes the foundation of a consciousness of increase [Bethsaidia]. We recognize that we have the ability to manifest our good from Universal Substance[e]. 45. As this 'engine of vigor and vitality' [our Philip quality] becomes more dynamic, it simulates our imagination [our Nathanael quality]. It is through our imagination that we can draw from the depths of our being [the Moses of us] great possibilities of forming Substance from the evolving awareness [Law] of our connection with Spirit. We begin to see that we can actualize our Christ qualities (our Jesusness), in spite of our sense-oriented mind [our Nazarian awareness]. To move Universal Substance from possibility to probability, we must elevate our unenlightened intellect to its spiritually sapient essence [the Joseph of us].

46. Initially we may question our ability to use our imagination

---

[e] *The quantum field of unmanifested possibility in potentia*

[our Nathanaelness] to draw Christed ideas from a sense-veneered consciousness [Nazareth]. However, we must trust the urges and promptings of our divinely-charged interior energies [the Philip of us] which receive their vibrancy from Spirit.

47. When we acknowledge our true nature (we are prompted by the Jesus of us), we can be sure that we are capable of using our imagination [our Nathanael quality] to produce an illumined idea [an Israelite]. Each such idea springs from a Christ-centered consciousness [is not false].

48. Even before our imagination [our Nathanael quality] becomes active, its presence-*in potentia* lies dormant in the recesses of our consciousness [is still under the fig tree]. To call it forward we must tap into the vital currents of our energetic power center [our Philip quality].

49. It is through the imaging power of the enlightened mind that we can connect with our inner wisdom. It is this connection which confirms that the Guiding Life Principle [Rabbi] is the Indwelling Cosmic Christ [Son of God]. Our quickening spiritual consciousness [King of Israel] is the unfoldment of actualizing that Christ connection.

50. Once we turn our latent spiritual energies [we are seen under the fig tree] into conscious engines of interior transformation, we shall be able to grasp incredible truths. 51. When we attain that purified state of Christed awareness [Heaven opens], our lives will be blessed with an extraordinarily attuned consciousness which is ultra-sensitive to Divine Ideas [angels] and is able to incorporate them in creative and formative ways [ascending and descending angels] to free our waking consciousness [our Son of manness] from error.

Chapter Two

The Wedding in Cana

1. When we are in a state of balanced spiritual energies [in Cana], we can move beyond the centrifugal force of our subconscious hang-ups and embedded (pediatric) theology [our Galilean perspective]. We discover that we can unite [wed] our human self with our Christ Self by demonstrating a high degree of love and intuitive receptivity [our Mary qualities] for the truth. Every level of our being – our body, mind, and soul [the third day] – is harmonized.

2. This harmonization is made possible when we consciously become one with the Pattern of Perfection [the Christ as Jesus] within us. All of our spiritual power centers [disciples] are vitalized.

3. When we fail to acknowledge our divinity [the wine is gone], our intuitive receptivity [our Mary quality] to our Christ connection senses the disconnect and we feel a lingering emptiness and growing dissatisfaction with our lives.

4. Although we are Christs potentializing, our Christhood is not quite actualized [my time has not come] at this stage of our spiritual unfoldment.

5. Nevertheless, our superior intuitive receptivity [the Mary of us] prepares our body, mind, and soul [servants] for their sacrosanct unfoldment ["Do whatever He tells you."].

6. We must guard against being too influenced by our five senses and an unenlightened intellect [six stone jars], which are prone to filter our experiences through the prism [ceremonial washing, rites of purification] of established religious dogmas [our Jewish regimentation] and sensory appetites. These "vessels" see duality and separation [symbolized by the number twenty] in everything [symbolized by the number thirty].

7. However, when we connect with the pattern of Christ perfection within us [our Christed Jesusness], an abun-

dance of vital energy [water] *pours* into our "perceptual vessels," (the five senses) elevating them to their highest expressions [filling them to the brim].

8. When our senses and intellect are lifted to their highest essences, we find we have the wherewithal to express that vitality [draw some out] as we move closer to transforming our Adamic consciousness [the master of the banquet] into its Cosmic Equivalent (Christ Consciousness).

9. As our Adamic (sense) consciousness unfolds toward its true nature, we sense that lower, more sense-connected energies [water] are being energetically charged with their higher, more spiritual essences [wine]. Even though we choose to remain products of our Adamic consciousness and cannot quite comprehend the transformation which is taking place [does not know where the wine originates], our body, mind, and soul [servants] are already feeling the effects of our potentialized Christ Nature [the bridegroom].

10. Up until now, our Adamic consciousness has been defined by its penchant for using spiritual truths [choice wine] for material gain [cheap wine]. This is particularly noticeable when our thoughts and attitudes [guests] are imbibed with sensory overload [have had too much to drink]. However, no matter how steeped in materiality we may be, we can elevate our sense-intoxicated thoughts to their higher, more spiritual natures [save the best for last].

11. By the time we reach this level of unfoldment, our vital energies have been transfused with their spiritually-charged counterparts [miraculous signs]. In this heightened state of spiritual equilibrium [Cana], we are able to overcome the spiritual inertia [Galilee] which defined our pre-Christed awareness. Having gotten a glimpse of our actualized Christ potential [glory], we fill our consciousness with thoughts [disciples]

which spring from a deeper inner knowing [faith]. This Spirit-filled knowing is fueled by the interior fermentation which is taking place.

Our Predictable Chemicalization

12. As we continue our spiritual unfoldment, we come to a place of genuine repentance [Capernaum], characterized by a yearning to cleanse our consciousness of all forms of error. We look forward to our transformation; we know that our evolving receptivity [our Mary quality] to our spiritual growth, our spiritually congruent thoughts [brothers], and our quickening spiritual qualities [disciples] will all work together to fortify our truth walk.

13. We realize it is time for us to move from our dependence on sense consciousness (coma consciousness) to the independence which comes from a spiritually-attuned consciousness [a process symbolized by the Jewish Passover experience]. To do this, we must go to that place of abiding peace within us [Jerusalem] to actualize our Christ potential [the Jesus of us]. 14. As we dutifully seek this interior transformation, we discover that our consciousness is filled with as many discordant materialistic thoughts [cattle and money] as there are spiritually-oriented thoughts [doves].

15. There begins to occur a depth charge of inner resolve [whips], which directs its biting transformative energies [cords] at inharmonious thoughts and pockets of discord. This intensity can lead to a rather volatile process of cleansing and purification. The fusion of enlightened thoughts and stale belief systems causes an internal emotional combustion, which sends specks and flecks of our ego's insecurities to the surface [drove all from the temple]. Our materialistic tendencies are uprooted [tables over-turned] and our dependence on man-made solutions dissolved [coins scat-

tered]. ¹⁶· Our resistance to spiritually-oriented ideas [doves] is erased. Toxic thoughts and bleaching beliefs which can contaminate our higher consciousness [Father's house] are forced out (detoxed) before they compromise our spiritual growth.

¹⁷· Although it is good to be enthusiastic about our spiritual growth, we must learn to bridle our zealousness. Over-zealousness may cause burnout [consume us] and dampen the progress we have made.

Upgrading Our Consciousness

¹⁸· If we are not careful, our purely religious biases [our Jewishness] will demand physical evidence of our spiritually-vitalized capacities [miraculous signs] to prove our connection to Spirit.

¹⁹· Because of our Christ potential [the Jesus of us], we are able to mitigate the debilitating effects of destructive thoughts which can weaken and even sever our conscious connection to our Christed thought system [temple]. We are able to revitalize [raise] our thought universe by filling our subconsciousness, consciousness, and super-consciousness [three days] with Christed thoughts, insights, and ideas.

²⁰· If we are merely the product of our religious beliefs and biases [our rigid Jewishness], we generally assume that our body is the aggregate [forty] of our five senses and intellect [five plus one equals six]. If we are stuck in this materialistically-inclined Adamic orbit, it will be difficult for us to comprehend the transformative power of a fully enlightened consciousness, subconsciousness, and super-consciousness [three days].

²¹· As we become more attuned to our spiritual nature, we realize that our true temple is our Christ Consciousness.

²²· When we elevate our waking consciousness to our Christ awareness [raise the dead], our quickened spiritual qualities [disciples] are transfused [believe] with the vital energies of Spirit.

23. This *upgrade* in awareness [a Passover experience] takes place when we are in a state of abiding inner peace and tranquility [Jerusalem]. Our entire constellation of thoughts [many people] is charged with spiritual oomph and vigor [miraculous signs]. 24. As we actualize our Christ potential [the Jesus of us], we have little difficulty discriminating between sense-coated thoughts and spiritually-consecrated thoughts [people].

25. There is no need to prove our spiritual worth [testimony is unnecessary]. We only need to express our true nature by elevating each incarnated *self*[a] to the Christ *Self*.

Chapter Three

Nicodemusian Obstetrics

1. There is a tendency within us, our fundamental religious perspective [the Nicodemus of us], to cling to encrusted theological biases and dogmas [our pharisaical bent]. Unfortunately, these dogmatic tendencies can define our over-all religious outlook [Jewish ruling council/Jewish leadership]. 2. Oftentimes religious fundamentalism shows up as spiritual darkness [came at night], because it springs from a belief in the letter of the law with little, if any, attention given to the spirit of the law. However, despite such myopic fundamentalism, we sense there is a remarkably prominent Guiding Principle [Rabbi] at work within us. The conscious realization of such guidance usually occurs when we experience the transfusion of immense spiritual energies [miraculous signs] within us. This seems to suggest the presence of the Eternal Isness [God, (the One Reality, the Absolute)] expressing Itself through the Cosmic Christ *as* us.

3. Be assured, we can only attain Christ Consciousness [the Kingdom of God] when we transcend sense appetites (coma

---
[a] *We experience many incarnations on our way to actualizing our Christhood.*

consciousness) and become consciously one with our Christ Self [be born again].

4. We may wonder how we can transcend [be born again] deeply engrained sense appetites and material propensities when we have been so fundamentally influenced by conventional religious programming. It is this attachment to religious parochialism and secular biases [a second time] that prevents us from awakening to our conscious unity with the Universal Isness through the Cosmic Christ [entering the womb to be born].

5. It is only through the potentializing power of our Christ potential [the Jesus of us] that we are able to attain Christ Consciousness [enter the Kingdom of God]. We must cleanse ourselves of worldly attachments [water] and strive to become one with the enthroned Christ [Spirit] within us. 6. Error [(desire for the) flesh (physicality)] perpetuates [gives birth to] error [flesh (incarnational experiences)], but our Christ Nature [Spirit] actualizes [gives birth again, (attains cosmic consciousness again)] our Christhood [Spirit]. 7. Clearly, we must transcend [be born again] our mindless attachments to materiality if we expect to become enlightened.

8. In the material universe it is difficult, but not impossible, for physical effects to precede their quantumly entangled causes. The same thing is true for human consciousness – to comprehend it has been underwritten [born] by God, the Eternal Isness [Spirit] even before we choose incarnational cycles to work on our untapped divinity. 9. As long as we remain the product of a sense-soaked consciousness [our Nicodemusian perspective], we will fail to comprehend our True Nature.

10. We have a consciousness which is warrantied by our *indivisible* connection with Spirit ["You are Israel's teacher"], and yet we choose to remain oblivious to our innate divinity. 11. Everyday we receive spirit-

filled insights [we speak of what we know] and intuit divine ideas [testify], but still fail to see the connection [do not accept the testimony] between our incarnated *self* and our Christ *Self*. 12. If we fail to comprehend worldly [earthly] truths, how can we possibly understand spiritual [heavenly] truths?

13. We will not become consciously one with the Christ Presence [heaven], which is our true state of being [one who came from heaven], until we are able to discern Truth from error [our Son of Man awareness]. 14. As we zealously unfold [our Mosesic resolve] toward our Christhood we raise our latent spiritual power centers (*kundalini* energies, the inner fire of the Holy Spirit). This *sushumnic* harmonics[a] is the cosmic result of the error erasure process [our Son of Man-ness]. 15. When we reach that level of unfoldment our entire consciousness [everyone] will have become Christed [have eternal life].

The Only Way to Eternal Life

16. God (the Eternal Isness, Absolute Good, the One Reality) manifests [so loved] Itself as the Cosmic Christ [Only Begotten Son] in human (Adamic) consciousness [the world], and whoever comes into that Christed awareness [believeth] will move beyond the illusion of separation and duality [will not die] and shall attain Christhood [eternal life].

The Presence of the Indwelling Cosmic Christ

17. God (Absolute Good, the One Reality, the Infinite Invisibleness) has not enfolded the Cosmic Christ [Only Begotten Son] into human consciousness [the world] to acknowledge error [condemn the world]. Instead, the Cosmic Christ is sent to *imprint the pattern of perfection* [save] in our consciousness [the world] so that we can cleanse our consciousness of error. 18. When we fill

---

[a] *Serpentine (kundalini) energies which radiate up from the base of the spine to the crown center at the top of the head.*

our consciousness with Christed thoughts [believe on Him], we make it clear that we do not endorse error [are not condemned]. But if we fail to fill our consciousness with Christed thoughts and intentions [do not believe], we create a sense-veneered consciousness [are condemned already] which is oblivious [does not believe] to the presence of the Indwelling Cosmic Christ [Only Begotten Son]. [19.] The truth is [the verdict], the Cosmic Christ [Light] is imprinted in human consciousness [the world], despite our choosing to ignore our Christ Connection [remain in darkness]. This disconnect becomes blatantly obvious when our actions spring from anti-Christed thoughts and inclinations [evil]. [20.] Whenever we choose error [evil] over Truth [light], we tend to rationalize our culpability by relinquishing responsibility for our anti-Christed actions. [21.] However, when we chose to apply Truth principles, we come into the awareness [light] that we are physical expressions of the Eternal Isness [God, (the One Reality)].

Bridling the Intellect

[22.] In the process of actualizing our Christ potential [the Jesus of us], our spiritual qualities [disciples] are raised to their higher essences. Our whole consciousness [countryside] is filled with Christed thoughts [Judea] and so many of our material inclinations are dissolved [baptism]. [23.] This natural inclination [plenty of water] toward inner peace [Salim] is the result of a spiritually attuned intellect [our John the Baptizer quality] which seeks to purge itself [baptize] from error. It is this inner resolve [our Aenon urge] to purify our consciousness that keeps us on the path of unfoldment. [24.] All of this is possible if we refuse to allow our quickening intellect [our John the Baptizer quality] to get hemmed in [imprisoned] by sense attachments.

25. As our spiritual inclinations [John's disciples] begin to blossom, we may be faced with worldly thoughts [our Jewish bent], which may cause us to question our empassioned consistency in removing [ceremonial washings] error thoughts from our consciousness. 26. In our attempt to spiritualize our intellect [they came to John], we must work through error beliefs that assume our intellect is the powerful guiding Presence [Rabbi] which transforms our subconscious energies [on the other side of the Jordon]. It is important to realize that the intellect, no matter how spiritually attuned, is unable to purge [baptize] the subconscious of deeply embedded error patterns.

27. An enlightened intellect [our John the Baptizer quality] indicates we know our limits. 28. We know the attuned intellect is the product of the self [I am not the Christ] and so we must prepare ourselves [be sent ahead] to raise the intellect to a more enlightened level of awareness. 29. The intellect's highest essence, superior intuition [bride], comes from [belongs to] our Christ Nature [bridegroom]. And a quickened intellect [the friend who attends the bridegroom] is fertile soil for higher spiritual understanding and can become fully illumined [hear the bridegroom's voice]. 30. Our spiritual awareness must dominate [become greater] our consciousness; and our intellect must be purged of sense-attachments [become less].

Christship Through Karmic Matriculation

31. A Christed thought [the one who comes from above] is a superior thought [is above all]. A thought [the one] which springs from Adamic consciousness [the earth] is a product of sense consciousness (coma consciousness). 32. The Christ Presence within us is our Cosmic Guarantor [testifies], and yet we tend to have thoughts of separation [fail to accept His

testimony]. [33.] On the other hand, if we dutifully grow a Christ Consciousness [accept His testimony] we will live, move, and have our being [certify] from the awareness that we are one with the Christ *as* us. [34.] We must understand that the Cosmic Christ, enfleshed as us [the One whom God has sent] has as one of Its essential characteristics a highly attuned Spiritual Will [speak the words of God] which is eternal [without limit/measure]. [35.] The Omnipresent Eternal Isness [the Father, (the Absolute, the Infinite Invisibleness)] expresses Itself [loves] as the Universal Cosmic Christ [the Son] which underwrites all physicality [all things placed in His hands]. [36.] When we resolutely strive toward our Christhood [believe in the Son], we shall attain Christ Consciousness [eternal life]. However, if we choose to remain attached to sense pleasures and material addictions [reject the Son], we will delay our Christhood [will not see life] until we suffer through what has been described as the dark night of the soul (the process of overcoming our sense attachments). This purging process is called karmic matriculation [the wrath of God].

Chapter Four

A Samaritan Moment

[1.] As we continue our spiritual growth, our old, established belief systems [our pharisaical thoughts] become purged [baptized] as we actualize our Christ potential [Jesus] and turn mere human qualities into their higher, more spiritual, counterparts [disciples]. [2.] It is our quickened spiritual qualities [disciples], which spring from our actualized Christ potential [our Jesusness], that raise [baptize] our awareness. [3.] Our continued unfoldment requires that both our super-conscious [Judea] and subconscious [Galilee] become Christized.

4. In order to do this, we must work through the spiritual reticence [Samaria] of a quickening, but sense afflicted-intellect. 5. We must come to the understanding [the Jacob of us] that our ability to conceive the imperceptible [our Josephness] depends on eliminating the disconnect [Sychar] between intellect and Spirit. 6. It is at the juncture [Jacob's well] of intellect and Spirit that our actualized Christ potential [the Jesus of us] holds the most promise. The inner harmonics [sixth hour] of our entire being is affected by the hydraulic relationship between intellect and Spirit.

7. Due to our unquickened emotional nature [the Samaritan woman], we see the spiritually aware, but as yet unawakened intellect [Jacob's well] as the answer [come to draw water] to mastering our human experience. However, both the intellect and our feeling nature have the potential to become Christed [Jesus asks for a drink]. 8. Our higher spiritual qualities [disciples] can draw out the best virtues [buy food] from even the most discordant co-dependence [Sychar] between an unawakened intellect and our unquickened feeling nature.

9. Emotionally, we recognize a spiritually-oriented thought [our enlightened Jewish perspective] from a spiritually reticent thought [our Samaritan disposition]. The dissonance between the two is obvious.

10. When we truly seek to attain Christ Consciousness [the Gift of God], we understand that our purely human qualities can be raised [are asked for a drink] to their higher spiritual essences. We have an opportunity for the conscious realization of eternal life [living water].

11. If we are the products of an unquickened intellect, despite being influenced by our quickening intuition, we are generally unable to grasp the depth of our spirituality [nothing with which to draw/no bucket]. We find it difficult to comprehend the Source of our greater good

[living water]. ¹². We also cannot comprehend that anything is superior to an intellectual understanding [Jacob] which seeks [drinks from] material answers to spiritual questions.

¹³. The truth of the matter is, when we depend only on the intellect's *gnosis* [drink from man-made wells], we will not comprehend hidden Truths [remain thirsty]. ¹⁴. On the other hand, when we seek to understand higher spiritual truths [drink the water], we will bypass the limitations of the intellect and access higher truths [never thirst]. Indeed our entire consciousness will be revitalized with the transformative amperage [spring water] of Spirit, which leads to our eventual Christship [eternal life].

¹⁵. At a deep emotional level, we begin to sense that we do not have to seek inner wisdom from external sources. ¹⁶. However, feelings alone will not suffice. We must allow our emotions and a quickened intellect [husband] to work in concert. ¹⁷. On a deep emotional level, we know a sense-veneered intellect is not capable of providing spiritual wisdom [we have no husband]. ¹⁸. In fact, an intellect which is merely the product of the five physical senses [five husbands] is not an enlightened intellect at all.

¹⁹. The intellect's inability to grasp the nuances of higher truths becomes obvious the more we examine the effects of spiritual laws [prophet]. ²⁰. As we begin to lead more spiritually-active lives, we may find that our previous inclinations [fathers/ancestors] toward finding spiritual clarity were characterized by intellectualizing [worshipping] our spirituality [mountain]. However, our spiritual growth requires that we pay attention to our Christed thoughts [our Jesus aspect], so that we focus on going to that place of abiding peace [Jerusalem] within.

²¹. It is important for us to know that we must move beyond religious formalities for formalities sake, thinking we must

erect material forms of worship to prove our spirituality. [22.] We get emotionally attached to external forms of worship and miss the interior meanings the external forms represent. Purging our consciousness from error [salvation] means elevating our ritualistically religious thoughts [our Jewish propensities] to their highest spiritual trajectories. [23.] It is the Christ-centered thoughts which transform us. [24.] The Eternal Isness [God, (the Absolute, the One Reality)] is the Abiding Omnipresence [Spirit] which underwrites all of our being and doing.

[25.] Until we understand our true relationship with the Christ [Messiah], we may believe in the religiophobic view of an external anthromoporphic God outside of us. [26.] However, we must realize that we are, in this now moment, expressions of the Cosmic Christ at the point of us.

[27] When our higher spiritual qualities [disciples] are attuned, it is surprising how receptive our feeling nature is to their energetic permeations. [28.] As we grow accustomed to this heightened awareness, we release pent-up emotions [leave the water jar] and are willing to erase former patterns of thought [town] that defined our thinking. [29.] We sense there is a Presence deep within us, a Perfect Pattern of Wholeness [the Christ] which underlies every thought, word, and action [knows everything we have ever done]. [30.] Our receptivity to this Presence changes our conventional thought processes [town] and we open ourselves to our higher spiritual nature.

Spiritual Soil

[31.] As we come into a more expanded awareness we begin to acquire the understanding [eat] that there is, in fact, a Guiding Principle [Rabbi] at work.

[32.] We also begin to sense that this Presence (the Christ) operates at a much deeper level of understanding [has food to eat]. We feel less a need to concern ourselves about material things.

33. Because our spiritual qualities [disciples] are still evolving, we are not yet quite able to grasp the omnipresent availability (the quantum field of possibilities) of Substance.

34. The deeper truths [food] that prepare us to actualize our Christ Potential [the Jesus of us] make it clear that the *out-formation* [will] of the Divine Pattern [the enthroned Christ] leads to the manifestation of our Christhood (the finished work). 35. As we prepare our physical, mental, emotional, and spiritual soil [four months] for our eventual Christhood [harvest], we must allow our spiritual qualities [the fields] to unfold, since, by their very nature, they are whole [ripe for harvest].

36. What we sow in consciousness [receive wages] becomes part of our human experience [harvest]. In truth, when we attain Christ Consciousness [eternal life], sowing and reaping [cause and effect] are one and the same [rejoice together/are glad together] at the level of Spirit.

37. When an enlightened mind [one] produces [sows] Christed thoughts, our entire consciousness [another] is raised [reaps] to its highest spiritual essence. 38. As we evolve [reap] into the conscious awareness of our Christ Nature, we discover that at a super-conscious level our higher thoughts [others] are already Christed [have done the hard/laborious work]. The truth is, at the core of our being, we are Christ enfleshed *as* us [reap the benefits of our labor].

Capitalizing on a Samaritan Moment

39. When we reach a certain level of adeptship, the spiritual reticence [our Samaritan awkwardness] which springs from former patterns of thought [town] loses its hold on us, because we realize that the essence of every thought, word, and action [everything ever done] has its foundation in Spirit. 40. Having lost our reticence [Samaritans come to Him], we seek to

harmonize our spiritual and human qualities [stayed two days].

41. As this inner process unfolds, truths realized in consciousness [world] create Christed thoughts [believers] which begin to permeate our waking consciousness.

42. Our initial emotional buy-in [the Samaritan women] matures to the point that we grasp [hear] inner truths because we surrender to (consciously become one with) the Cosmic Christ [Savior] expressing Itself quantumly as us.

Bookmarking Our Faith With Action

43 Once we have harmonized our spiritual and human qualities [two days], our subconscious energies [Galilee] are also transformed. 44. However, we must move beyond the illusion of our own insignificance [have no honor] when it comes to the spiritual origins and power of our evolving consciousness [country]. 45. When we pay attention to the latent energies in our subconscious [arrive in Galilee], we can take steps to transform them [the Galileans welcomed Him] by consciously freeing ourselves from old thought patterns [the Passover experience] so we can *keynote* each day with affirmations of inner peace [go to Jerusalem].

46. Because we are in a state of balanced spiritual energies [Cana], we can transfuse our subconscious hang-ups and thought patterns [Galilee] with vital currents of thought [water] by elevating them into their higher spiritual essences [wine].

46. This transformation is possible because there is that within us, an abiding conviction of the restorative powers of Spirit [a Capernaum revelation], which knows that a highly spiritualized thought [royal official] can replace a sense-veneered thought [sick son].

47. When a spiritually-attuned thought is raised to its highest vibration [Jesus arrives in Galilee from Judea], it can literally turn

John 4, 5

spiritual unawareness [death] into Christed awareness. [48.] It is important to note that an unenlightened mind seeks confirmation of inner growth through external proofs [signs/wonders].

[49.] However, an enlightened perspective produces highly spiritualized thoughts [the royal official]. Because of our unwavering faith, we know that any sense-coated thought [sick son near death] [50.] can be raised to its spiritual essence [the son will live]. It is from a consciousness of expectation and reverence [he took Jesus at His word] that we can step out on faith [the man departed]. [51.] When we bookmark our faith with action, we find that any doubts [servants] we may have had give way to our manifested good [the boy lives]. [52.] Because there is no geography in Spirit, the moment we affirm our good the *seed* for its perfect manifestation [the seventh hour] has been created (as above, so below).

[53.] When we live at the speed of faith, our thoughts are raised to their highest spiritual essences [the son lives] and our entire consciousness [household] is filled with Christed energies.

[54.] At this point in our evolving awareness, both our intellect and emotions are harmonized and transfused into their spiritual counterparts [the second miraculous sign]. This happens every time spiritualized ideas [Judea] penetrate our subconscious [Galilee].

Chapter Five

Our Anemic Bethesdaic Awkwardness

[1.] As we continue to actualize our Christ potential [the Jesus of us], we realize that whenever we go to that place (still point) of abiding peace [Jerusalem] within us, we have immediate access to the omnipresent substance [feast] which can be materialized by quickened thought power [our spiritually aware

Jewishness]. 2. Our unfoldment depends on our willingness to allow the healing flow of divine ideas from our super-conscious reservoir [pool] of ideas to penetrate our conscious and subconscious filters. Centering ourselves in the peace [Jerusalem] which passes all *mis*understanding, we create a psychic channel [Sheep Gate] for Christed thoughts to bathe our senses [five porticoes/colonnades] with healing (wholing) energies. 3. At this stage of our unfoldment, there are a great *multitude* of sick and infirmed thoughts [disabled people] which have not been raised to their highest spiritual essences.

4. However, when a highly spiritualized thought [angel of God] enters our consciousness [baptismal pool], it creates an energetic reaction in our thought currents [stirs up the waters]. Spiritualized thoughts influence future thoughts by elevating them to their higher spiritual essences (heal them of *dis-ease*).

5. What usually happens is there is at least one well-established, although limited, thought pattern [an invalid], which is the product of sense consciousness (coma consciousness). This anemic thought pattern affects the harmonics of both our human and spiritual aspects [represented by the number thirty-eight, which is 3 + 8 or 11]. 6. The question we must ask ourselves is, how long do we want to allow discordant thoughts to pollute our consciousness with *sense sludge?*

7. If our consciousness is not grounded in Spirit [no one to help me], our sense-veneered thoughts (affirmaties) will not be able to correct the disequilibrium [the water is stirred] caused by such infirmed thinking. Consequently, we quarantine ourselves from the quantum field [pool] of divine ideas.

8. The truth is, when we affirm our oneness with Spirit, we can move beyond [pick up our mat] any and all human limitations which we have allowed to

immobilize us. Consequently, we can claim wholeness [able to walk]. 9. Each time we affirm our wholeness, we establish the inner harmonics it takes to unite [cure] body, mind, and spirit. This *at-one-ment* [a Sabbath experience] which unites our *self* with our *Self* is simply one thought, one intention, one choice away. 10 We must move past established religious perspectives [our Jewish propensity] and narrowly-focused intellectual biases [the invalid who was healed] which limit our conscious *at-one-ment* [the Sabbath] with our True Self.

11. We must make it a daily practice to affirm our innate wholeness and oneness with Spirit. 12. Otherwise, we may question our heirship. 13 If we are not careful, an unquickened intellect may lose its appreciation for our innate divine connection [Jesus slips away] by reverting to old thought patterns [the crowd].

14. However, when we raise our consciousness [Jesus found him at the temple], we become consciously one with Spirit [are well again]. On the other hand, when we limit our spiritual growth [sin] we delay our enlightenment. 15. We must move beyond worldly thoughts [our unenlightened Jewishness] which promote cosmetic churchianity and, instead, embrace thoughts which characterize our knowing that we are innately divine [the enlightened Jesus of us].

Our Eternal Heirship Recognized

16. Any time we enter into a spiritually active mindset [a Sabbath experience] we generally become aware of intruding thoughts that come from old established religious perspectives [our Jewish propensity], and feel tempted [persecuted] to neglect our spiritual practice. 17. However, when we chose to focus on our Christ potential [the Jesus of us], we realize that the I-Amness [Father, (the One Reality, Divine Mind)] is omnipresent [always at work] and that we can

chose to honor that omnipresence [we can work, too]. [18.] As we continue to grow spiritually, stale religious beliefs [our Jewish rigidity] will surface which deny [seek to kill] our divine heirship. These thoughts spring from an unenlightened and paranoid us who not only fears a spiritually alive mindset [the Sabbath], but is traumatized at the prospect of our coming to the realization that we are the Christ (the Cosmic Christ) expressing at the point of us. We hamper our spiritual growth by remaining unaware that the Cosmic Christ is God [the Father, (the Infinite Invisibleness, the Absolute)] expressing Itself as the Cosmic Christ.

[19.] As we unfold our Christ potential [our Jesusness], we clearly see [I tell you the Truth] that the Cosmic Christ [the Son] is the formative aspect [can only do what the Father does] of the Eternal Isness [Father, (the One Reality)]. The Cosmic Christ and the Eternal Isness [Father, (the Absolute)] are one and the same. They are *indivisible*. [20.] The Eternal Isness [the Father, (the Infinite Invisibleness)] expresses Itself as the Cosmic Christ [loves the Son] and underwrites our Adamic consciousness [sense consciousness] with Christ potential. It is because of this Christ potential that we can bathe our human experience with Christ-centered thoughts, words, and actions [sense greater things]. [21.] It is because of the presence of the Eternal Isness [the Father, the One Reality)] within us that we can turn total unawareness of our divinity [raise the dead] into the Christed awareness [life] of our eternal nature.

[22.] When we elevate our consciousness to a super-conscious level, there is no need to discern Truth from error [the Father judges no one] because all of our thoughts are Christed. However, at the level of our Adamic consciousness (sense consciousness), there is much work to do to align ourselves with the Indwelling Christ [Son] which is ever vigilant [entrusted with judgment] [23] in guiding us to our greater good. When we purposefully seek this alignment with our Christ Nature [honor the Son], we become consciously one with [honor] the Eternal Isness [Father, the Infinite Invisibleness)]. If we neglect or deny [fail to honor] our innate divinity [the Son], we will remain oblivious [fail to honor] to the Source [Father] of our eternal life (Christ Consciousness).

[24.] Whenever we center ourselves in prayer [hear the word] and become consciously one with the Christ Presence within us [believe in him who sent me], we will move toward attaining Christ Consciousness [eternal life] and receive clemency [will not be condemned] for our pre-Christed thoughts and actions. This is what happens when we elevate our consciousness from its Adamic, sense-soaked state to its higher super-conscious orbit [crossed over/passed from death to life].

[25.] There will come a time in our spiritual unfoldment when we develop such a highly-attuned spiritual resolve [hear the voice of the Son of God] that we will outgrow any hesitance about expressing our divinity [the dead hear]. [26.] It is from this Christed perspective that we will see that all beingness [life] comes from the Eternal Isness [Father, (the One Reality, the Absolute)], and that the unmanifest becomes manifest [granted] through the formative power of the Cosmic Christ [the Son]. [27.] Through our eternal heirship, we are blessed with the wherewithal to free our soul (our human personality) from error (the illusion of separation and duality) by fully demonstrating our conscious oneness with Spirit (the Christ as us). This consciousness of oneness [our Son of Man quality] places us in a higher *orbit* of spiritual awareness [gives us authority to judge].

[28.] As we continue to expand our awareness, we will have

many opportunities to transform stale thoughts and beliefs [all who are in graves] into their highly attuned spiritual counterparts [those who hear his voice]. 29. Those perspectives and beliefs which we truly want to elevate [those who have done good] depend on our desire to raise them to their higher essences [live]. Those perspectives which are still the products of sense-sludge [have done evil] will have to be transformed into their higher spiritual essences through disciplined study and faithful actions.

Spiritual Attunement or Atrophy

30 Our Christ potential is just that – Christ potential ["By myself I can do nothing."]. It must be actualized. And so we must discern Truth from error based on our current understanding [what we hear] of truth principles. When we live, move, and have our being from a Christed perspective [good judgment], we have moved beyond the narcissism of the ego and demonstrated our conscious oneness with Spirit (the Cosmic Christ) through our thoughts, choices, words, and actions.

31. If we give ourselves sole credit for our spiritual unfoldment [testify about myself], we are merely legends in our own minds [our testimony is invalid]. 32. However, there is a Higher Essence (the Cosmic Christ) enthroned in us [which testifies on our behalf] which is our True Self [is a valid testimony].

33. An enlightened intellect [our John the Baptizer quality] acknowledges [testifies] that our True *Self* (the Cosmic Christ) is greater than our human *self*. 34. It is important to understand that the Truth is the Truth, regardless of what our ego [human testimony] believes or is able to comprehend. Serious adeptship demands that we cleanse our consciousness of error [be saved].

35 It is also important to realize that an enlightened intellect [our John the Baptizer quality] is able to shed only a certain amount of light when it comes to under-

standing spiritual truths. 36. While an illumined intellect [our John the Baptizer quality] is a prerequisite for greater spiritual understanding, our unfoldment depends on how well we actualize our Christ potential [the work that needs to be finished]. 37. It is the eternal formless I-Am Presence (God the Father, the Absolute, the One Reality) within us that exerts Its perennial *tug* (the still small voice), inviting us to awaken to our divinity. 38. If we allow ourselves to remain products of a fractured ego, we will not recognize our spiritual potential, let alone our True Nature.

39. No matter how versed we are in scripture, no matter how much we study the letter of the law, no matter how well we value literal interpretations of scripture – these alone, or combined, will not lead to Christ Consciousness [eternal life]. 40. Getting stuck at a superficial level of awareness will not help us to unfold into our Christhood.

41. We must move beyond an Adamic consciousness (sense consciousness) which produces sense-coated thoughts, concepts, and beliefs [humans/men] and live sacred scriptures from the inside-out. 42. If we remain stuck at a superficial level of unfoldment, we will not be able to see the wholeness or the underlying harmony [love of God] which permeates the physical universe.

43. We must become very clear about this: at the very core of our being we are divine. By our very nature [in His name], we are *indivisible* expressions of God [Father, (the One Reality, Divine Mind)] at the point of us. If we fail to grasp that Truth, we will remain in the grip of an egocentric personality determined to perpetuate its narcissistic dominance. 44. Sense thoughts lead to sense inclinations, which lead to sense appetites, which lead to sense choices, which lead to a chronic case of coma consciousness (a sense-soaked Adamic consciousness).

45. Lack of spiritual progress comes from our disconnect with Spirit (the Cosmic Christ in ex-

pression). When we cultivate this kind of ego-driven *portfolio,* it takes a considerable amount of self-examination and soul chemicalization (body, mind, and emotional purification) to pull ourselves out of the *spiritual atrophy* we have created [the Moses effect]. 46. When we recover from this predictable *chemicalization* [believe Moses], we will be able to lift our incarnated *self* (our human personality) out of its errancy into its spiritually awakened *Self.* 47. If we give in to our sense appetites [do not believe what Moses wrote], we will find it very difficult to actualize our Christhood.

Chapter Six

Transforming the Five Senses (Feeding the 5000)

1. When we recognize our unity with all life, it is the outformation of our clarity of vision (Sea of Tiberius) and the ability to rise above old patterns of thought (Sea of Galilee). 2. When we reach a certain level of unfoldment, our vital energies (the crowd) rise to their spiritually-charged counterparts (miraculous signs) as we continue our wholing (healing) process. 3. It is important to know that our spiritual qualities (disciples) are amplified every time we connect with our True Self through prayer and meditation (go up into the mountainside). 4. Our degree of unfoldment is determined by how well we move from one *cusp of consciousness* to another (the Passover experience).

5. We must continually remind ourselves that we have the power (our Philip quality) to turn the formless into the formed (bread). Our ability to do this is a simple matter of understanding and faith. 6. We must trust in our ability to demonstrate substance. 7. The power to manifest our good (our Phillipness) is based on solid spiritual ground (eight months of wages), a foun-

8. When our inner strength (the Andrew of us) is fortified by faith (our Simon Peter quality), 9. we will be able to move beyond the limitations imposed by our five senses (five loaves of bread) and maximize the creative potential (child) of our thinking and feeling natures (two fish).

10. If we trust in our ability to fully become aware of our Christ potential (the Jesus of us), we will feel grounded (sit on the grass) in Truth and better able to transform the physical senses (5,000 is 5 amplified) into awesome receptors [conduits] of Truth. 11. The more we give thanks for our connection with Spirit, the more prosperity we will enjoy.

12. When we truly understand (eat) the truth of who we really are, we will elevate our awareness to a spiritually alive state of consciousness, instead of settling for a materially wasted state of consciousness. 13. As we continue to raise our awareness, all twelve of our spiritual faculties (twelve baskets) will become so enriched that our physical senses (five barley leaves) will become enriched as well.

14. Once our thoughts are in alignment with higher spiritual laws (miraculous signs), it becomes clear to us that the Cosmic Christ (the Prophet) is enfleshed *as* us (the world). 15. Although we are one with the Indwelling Christ, we must remember that Christ potential is not the same thing as actualized Christ potential.

Walking on Water

16. Occasionally, we may experience times when we seem spiritually unreceptive (evening). However, even in those times our spiritual qualities (disciples) permeate existing pockets of negativity (lake). 17. We must realize that a positive mindset (boat) keeps us connected to an abiding current of natural healing (Capernaum), which sustains us

until we sense our innate Christ potential (the Jesus of us). [18.] When strong currents of negativity surface (a strong wind), we may give in to our emotions (rough waters/seas). [19.] If we depend only on our human abilities (row), no matter how resourceful or creative (symbolized by three; three-and-a half; or three or four) they may be, we will fail to appreciate the power of our actualized Christ potential (the Jesus of us) to elevate us above negativity (walking on water).

[20.] We must remind ourselves that we are the Christ expressing at the point of us. [21.] It is that awareness which will help us rise above any and all negativity (take him in the boat) so we can master the art of living (the boat reaches the shore).

The Bread of Life

[22.] As we come to a higher state of awareness (the next day), our thoughts (crowd), which are still attached to materiality (are on the opposite shore), are mediated by the awareness that we are responsible for our mindsets (boat) and life choices. Developing our Christ potential (the Jesus of us) is up to us (Jesus had not entered the boat). We already have the spiritual wherewithal (disciples) to rise above perceived lack and limitation. [23.] Once we grasp the full implications of our innate divinity (see boats from Tiberius), it becomes clear that we already have an innate understanding of the omnipresence of unlimited supply (have eaten the bread). [24.] Spirit won't do for us what we are unwilling to do for ourselves. We must surrender to the abiding presence of wholeness (go to Capernaum) if we expect to master the human experience.

[25.] When we fill our consciousness with positive, spiritually-charged thoughts (go to the other side of the lake), we discover that our Christ potential (Rabbi) has always been a core facet of our being.

26. Unfortunately, many of us satisfy our spiritual curiosity (eat loaves of bread) from an intellectual standpoint, instead of experiencing the spiritually-charged transformative effects [miraculous signs] that come from practicing the Presence. 27. We must not seek to satisfy overly-consumptive material appetites (food that spoils/perishes), but strive to understand universal truths (food that endures). Our unfolding Christ Consciousness (eternal life) depends on our ability and interest in discerning Truth from error (our Son of Man quality). This innate spiritual wiring is our birthright (seal of approval) and comes from the Christ of us, which is the formative aspect of the Eternal Isness (God, the Father, the One Reality) which underwrites both the manifest and unmanifest realms of being.

28. We may wonder how we can achieve Christhood, 29. but the answer is obvious: Because we are spiritual beings endowed with awesome Christ potential (our Jesus aspect), we have only to surrender to (awaken to) our Higher Self, which is the Cosmic Christ.

30. Until we fully embrace the Truth of our Indwelling Christ Self, we will tend to look for evidence 'out there' instead of experiencing the transformative energies within. 31. We will look for spiritual sustenance (manna) through old filters (forefathers), which will keep our spirituality arid and sterile (desert).

32. The following Truth cannot be put any more clearly: It is not us who draws Universal Substance (bread) to us (our Mosaic nature), because we are not the source of that substance. What happens is we raise our consciousness [expand our awareness] to a Christed level, one which is attuned to omnipresent Universal Supply. To put it simply, Universal Substance doesn't come to us; we go to it. 33. The Cosmic Christ (the True Bread of God) is the formative power of the Eternal

Isness (Father, the One Reality). It is the Cosmic Christ which underwrites our physical existence so that we can comprehend eternal truths (the bread of life).

34. When we truly comprehend Universal Truths, we will want to learn, and then apply, truth principles which help us expand our awareness.

35. When we actualize our Christhood (as Jesus did), we will discover that we are flesh and blood expressions (quantum editions) of Eternal Truths (the bread of life). We will have mastered the human experience (never hunger or thirst). 36. However, much too often, we simply intellectualize (see) our heirship instead of feeling it (believe) from a body, mind, and soul perspective. 37. At the level of Spirit [Father, (the Absolute, the One Reality)], we are already Christed beings. Our 'skin school' task is to recognize that cosmic connection.

38. The Cosmic Christ becomes enfleshed, suffering the limitations associated with physicality (not his will), in order to reverse our self-imposed descent into the limitations of matter so we can become the best Christs we can be (the will of him who sent me), until we shed the desire for incarnational experiences.

39. This Truth is so important it must be repeated: The Will of God (the Infinite Invisibleness) is that, through the activity of the Cosmic Christ, all living things will be restored to their Christed state (the last day).

40. Once again: The Will of God [Father, (the Absolute)] is that we become the best Christs we can be [look to the Son], so that we can achieve Christhood (eternal life). That means erasing all illusions of duality and separation from our consciousness, so we can completely unfold into our Christ awareness (raise him up) by transcending our mortal consciousness (the last day).

41 Until we are at the point on our Truth walks where we

fully express our divinity, we may find, from time-to-time, that purely dogmatic thoughts [our worldly Jewish bents] may surface. These dogmatic propensities may cause us to question the value of eternal truths (bread from heaven). 42. If we do not understand the connection between our illumined intellect (the Joseph of us) and superior intuition (our Mary quality) which produce the awareness of our Christ potential (the Jesus of us), we will fail to grasp our capacity for enlightenment (heaven).

43. We must move beyond our dogmatic tendencies. 44. We will not actualize our Christ potential unless we realize we are divine expressions of God (the Father, the One Reality), which manifests Itself as the Cosmic Christ in the physical universe. Once we have that Christed realization, we will have transcended the limitations of mortal awareness (be raised up at the last day).

45. When we raise our awareness (it is written in the Prophets) to the Christ realization (taught by God), we will undoubtedly apply Truth principles (listen to God, the Father) which keep us centered on our Truth walks. 46. On the other hand, we will not become fully Christed (see the Father) unless we acknowledge our innate divinity (one who is from God) and apply Truth principles (see the Father).

47. There is no shortcut to enlightenment. We must apply the truths we know (believe) to unfold into our Christ Consciousness (everlasting life). 48. We can become flesh and blood expressions of Eternal Truths (the bread of life) if we take our spiritual growth seriously.

49. If we look for spiritual sustenance (manna) through old, stale belief systems (forefathers), we will miss (die) underlying eternal truths. 50. But when we apply the eternal truths (bread) which spring from a Christed consciousness (heaven), we will understand [eat] the nature of eternal truths [will not die]. 51. When we become conscious

expressions of eternal truths [bread from heaven], we will attain Christ Consciousness (live forever). Eternal truths (bread) are essentially spiritual laws expressed in their physical forms (flesh), which can be applied through disciplined practice to elevate our consciousness [world].

52. As has been mentioned before, until we fully express our divinity, our dogmatic, invective nature [our Jewish propensity] causes us to question the value of spiritual laws encased in matter (flesh), which we may consider to be foreign to our belief system.

53. We must understand this incontrovertible universal truth: Unless we comprehend the nature of eternal truths [eat the flesh], discern truth from error [our Son of Man capacity], and grasp our unity with Spirit [drink his blood], we will not move any closer to our Christship (life).

54. When we comprehend eternal truths [eat flesh] and grasp our *indivisibleness* with Spirit [drink blood], we will attain Christ Consciousness [eternal life]. We will move beyond the inertia of mortal consciousness [be raised up at the last day].

55. Eternal truths [flesh] are spiritual food, and conscious realization of our divinity [blood] is spiritual unity [drink].

56. When we understand [eat] eternal truths [flesh] and comprehend our unity with our Christ Self [drink blood], it becomes clear to us that we are *indivisible* expressions of the Cosmic Christ.

57. Just as the Cosmic Christ is the formative aspect of the Eternal Isness (Father, the One Reality), quantumly speaking, we are the physical expressions of the Cosmic Christ, spiritually speaking.

58. At the risk of seeming redundant, the following truth is so essential it must be repeated: Our *indivisibleness* with the Cosmic Christ is an eternal truth [bread], and it comes from a Christed consciousness [heaven]. If we follow purely religious teachings (manna) which spring from

primitive theology [forefathers], we will miss [die] underlying eternal truths. However, when we religiously follow eternal truths [eat bread], we will attain Christhood [eternal life]. [59.] We can come to this realization once we move beyond limited religious perspectives [the synagogue] and center ourselves in the abiding peace and serenity [Capernaum] of Spirit (the Eternal Isness, the One Reality).

Moving From Sense Appetites to Spiritual Aspirations

[60.] As we seek to comprehend hidden spiritual truths, many of our existing, more conventionally-coated thoughts and belief systems [disciples] will find these truths difficult to grasp. [61.] As we become aware of the myopic limitations associated with sense-burdened thoughts (immature disciples), we recognize how much our mortal consciousness (coma consciousness) inhibits the growth of our Christ potential (the Jesus of us). [62.] What if we mastered our ability to discern Truth from error [the Son of Man ascending] at the human level of consciousness? [63.] God, as the Cosmic Christ (the Only Begotten Son), also expresses Itself as the Holy Spirit, which animates [gives life] our 'skin school' experience. Our physical beingness itself (flesh) is ephemeral, temporal (counts for nothing/is useless), and is the product of sense consciousness. [64.] It is not difficult to see that sense-veneered thoughts are the offspring of our human personality, which tends to choose sense appetites [betray] over spiritual aspirations. [65.] It is because of this human tendency to discount our True nature that we allow ourselves to remain in darkness. Only through an awakened consciousness can we comprehend our I-Am-ness [the Father, (the One Reality, the Absolute)].

[66.] Unless we come to that realization, most of our thoughts and beliefs [disciples] will remain unquickened and energetically beneath their divine horizon. [67.] We may even question the spiritual viability and worth of the spiritual qualities [twelve disciples] we have already begun to quicken. [68.] Whenever these kinds of doubts surface, we must step out on faith [our Simon Peter quality] and recognize that we can attain Christ Consciousness [eternal life]. [69.] We must truly believe that the same Christ (Cosmic Christ) that expressed Itself as Jesus [the man from Nazareth] is the same Christ (Cosmic Christ) that expresses Itself as us.

[70.] Because of the nature of our physicality (having chosen human form and, thus, subject to the temptations of human experience) we will, at best, quicken our core spiritual qualities [twelve disciples] and, at the least, allow ourselves to succumb to the temptations associated with sense consciousness (our devilish, self-aggrandizing thoughts which deny our divinity; in short, our materialistic Judasness).

[71.] It is our self-aggrandizing nature [our warped Judas penchant] which springs from a purely acquisitive, selfish, overly-ambitious side of us [our Simon Iscariot nature] that is prone to compromise [betray] our spiritual growth.

Chapter Seven

The Undertone of Unbelief

[1.] It is interesting to note that when a Christed idea [the life of Jesus the Nazarene] penetrates our subconscious [Galilee], it is difficult for us to receive it openly [Jesus purposefully avoided Judea] if our current belief system is framed around encrusted religious beliefs and biases [our immature Jewishness]. This fractured perspective prompts us to negate [kill] the value of spiritually-charged thoughts. [2.] However, when we raise our awareness to a Christed orbit, we allow ourselves to move beyond the rigid limitations associated with our worldly personality, which is filled with sense addictions [the Feast of Tabernacles]. 3. Until we mature into our spirituality, there may be times when our rudimentary inclinations [brothers] demonstrate our impatience in forcing greater expressions of the divine powers we believe we have [go to Judea prematurely]. At this stage of our spiritual growth, we have not fully grasped the nature of higher spiritual laws [miracles]. 4. We fail to recognize that our adeptship is purely an inside-out process [acting in secret] which gets its vibrancy from an interior connection to Spirit, and not from external sense attachments [the world]. 5. We must transform our rudimentary perceptions [brothers] into refined spiritual insights.

6. Unless we gain a Christed outlook [our Jesus perspective], our Truth walks will only produce a superficial level of understanding. 7. A material consciousness [the world] loves material thoughts and cannot see the contamination caused by error [evil]. 8. Although we may want to move beyond the limitations inherent in a transient human perspective [the Feast], we are not quite ready to handle the inner changes which characterize our Christ Nature. 9. At this stage in our growth, there is much more integration and harmonization of energies which must take place in our consciousness. The transformative effects of the Embodied Christ must have time to do their work [He (Jesus) stays in Galilee].

Removing Error From Our Consciousness

10. Although it will not be immediately obvious, Spirit will do Its work [He went in secret], despite our being distracted by unrefined thoughts [brothers] that keep us mired in the false security of sense appetites [the Feast].

11. In our unrefined thinking, we have not yet gained the clarity to understand our true nature. 12. As our awareness develops, we sense there is more to hidden esoteric wisdom than we are able to grasp. And yet, we are still hesitant to abandon our preconceived notions of what it means to be enlightened. 13. We are not quite ready to abandon established religious habits and biases [our Jewish rigidity].

14. When our subconscious error patterns become conscious realizations [the *halfway point*[a] through the Feast], we can transcend their negative influence. 15. In this state of unrefined thinking, it may still be difficult for us to release our attachment to encrusted religious biases [our Jewish penchant] and the myopic effects of embedded (pediatric, cosmetic) theology. We generally find it difficult to grasp that a fully Christed life is our divine birthright.

16. The deepening awareness [teaching] of our innate divinity comes from acknowledging the presence of the Cosmic Christ within us *as* us. 17. When we choose to become the best Christ we can be [God's Will for our human incarnation], we know in our heart-of-hearts that we are expressions of the Cosmic Christ in human form. 18. However, because we have the power of choice, we can use the inner teachings for selfish personal gain and aggrandizement, or we can apply the teachings to honor our connection with Spirit. 19. What is important to know is that when we liberate ourselves from error [Moses gives the law], we must honor the liberation or it isn't true liberation [we fail to keep the law]. The question we must ask ourselves is: why do we deny [kill the commitment] our innate divinity? 20. If we are not careful, we will fall into the trap of justifying our error proneness [being demon possessed] by denying [killing] our innate divinity. Our materialistic thoughts

---

[a] *Generally speaking, our three states of consciousness as spiritual beings in physical form are: subconscious, waking conscious, super-conscious.*

[crowd] are the result of materialistic inclinations, and so we are tempted to view our experiences from that limited perspective.

21. We must remember that our Christ potential [the Jesus of us] expresses Itself as the undivided wholeness [one] of a higher spiritual dynamic [miracle/work], of which our materialistic minds cannot grasp.
22. Yet, as we attempt to liberate ourselves from error [our Mosaic penchant], we may not see the relationship between our current attempts at cutting our materialistic ties [circumcision], and our noble past efforts [patriarchs] to erase error from our consciousness. As a result, we may mistakenly censure [circumcise] a visible expression of our Christ potential [child], because we fail to see its relevance as an indicator of our purposeful detachment from material appetites [a Sabbath experience].
23. In terms of our spiritual growth, we must be able to discern the difference between freeing ourselves [circumcising] from a newly formed religious insight [child], which is the product of an unrefined moralistic nature, and its higher, more inclusive, spiritual counterpart, which is the product of our having raised our entire awareness [the whole man] to its Christed orbit. It is important to note that both of these perspectives, the religious and the spiritual, are part of the growth process we seek to separate ourselves from material pursuits [a Sabbath experience].
24. We must stop giving power to outer appearances, and declare our dominion over any and all perceived limitations.

The Limitations of a 'Skin School' Perspective

25. If our thoughts [people] are more religious than spiritual when we refrain from material pursuits [a Sabbath experience], we are liable to deny [kill] the full expression of our divine potential. 26. Even as we become more conscious [speak

publicly] of our innate divinity, our sense-veneered ego and ego-propelled intellect [authorities] are incapable of comprehending our *indivisible* connection with the Indwelling Christ. 27. If we allow an unenlightened ego and intellect to rule, we will see ourselves as mere flesh and blood human beings. In other words, the Christ *as* us is a difficult truth to grasp from a *skin school* (incarnated human) perspective.

28. Our Christ potential [the Jesus of us] always remains vibrant [is still teaching] within our waking consciousness [temple courts]. We may suspect from an unillumined perspective that we may be divine beings, but the truth of that heirship will remain obscured because, from an egocentric mindset, we are unable to comprehend or appreciate our true stature as flesh and blood expressions of the Cosmic Christ. 29. Once our religious nature matures by becoming more spiritual, we realize that we are spiritual beings who have chosen a human experience, which in and of itself does not mean we are separate from Spirit.

30. As has been mentioned previously, an unenlightened ego and its obedient intellect fail to grasp [try to seize] our true nature. 31. However, many highly spiritual thoughts and inclinations [crowd] will surface as we continue our truth walks. Deep within us there is a sense that when we fully realize our Christ potential, we will be able to turn catastrophic situations into benestrophic outcomes [miracles signs].

Handcuffed By a Warped Religiosity

32. If we stay fixated on purely literal interpretations of scripture and view the visible universe as sacrosanct [our pharisaical bent], we will find that esoterical thoughts [whispering crowd] make us uneasy. Unless we become more inclusive in our thinking and open to the guidance of Spirit, we may tend to

entrench ourselves in stale beliefs systems [chief priests and Pharisees], which are characterized by rigid parochial biases [temple guards/police] that dampen [arrest] our enthusiasm for anything which falls outside of those parameters, especially sacred knowledge.

33. When we faithfully seek to Christize our consciousness, we can abbreviate certain aspects of our unfoldment toward our Christ potential [the Jesus of us] by accelerating our demonstration of it. Our journey to become a fully accomplished Christ [the One which sent me] is a journey of disciplined volition. Our very next Christed thought, Christed choice, or Christed action can elevate us to a greater awareness of our Christhood.

34. We allow a sense-addicted ego (our Adamic consciousness) and its protégé, an unenlightened intellect, to prevent us (seek but not find) from comprehending our *indivisibleness* with our Christ Nature. 35. If we are the product of encrusted religious biases [our Jewishness], we will hide behind walled religious beliefs [the Greek of us] and use them to justify our 'gated' biases. 36. Unless we ease ourselves out of our warped religiosity, we will remain handcuffed by a recalcitrant ego and childish intellect intent on truncating our spiritual progress.

The Cleansing Power of Christed Thought Currents

37. Be assured that when we overcome our sense attachments and addictions [the last and greatest day of the Feast], we will feel the harmonics of our Christ potential [the Jesus of us] inviting us to immerse ourselves in the goodness of our Godness. 38. When we allow our Christ nature to express Itself [let whomever believes in me drink], our consciousness will be filled with Christed thought currents [rivers of living water] which bathe our consciousness with light and cleanse our thought

pathways of error. [39.] At this stage in our development, we have not sufficiently attuned ourselves with the omniactivity of the Holy Spirit [the Spirit was not yet given], because we have not fully realized our Christ potential [Jesus is not yet glorified].

Sorting Out Our Divine Genogram

[40.] As we become more spiritually inclined, some of our thoughts [crowd] may be the result of a clairvoyant [prophetic] capacity. We sense there is more to us than mere flesh and blood. [41.] We may have other thoughts which spring from our subconscious [Galilee] that question our worthiness and capacity to manifest our Christ Nature [our Messianic inheritance]. [42.] As we attempt to sort out our divine heritage [scriptural proof], especially our Messiahship, we realize that, at our core essence, we have been anointed with the love [our Davidic quality] of the Eternal Isness (God, the One Reality) *indivisibilized* as us. Our descent into human form is fused with divine energies which come from the unlimited and perpetually expansive[b] spiritual substance [Bethlehem] of God essence. [43.] Until we fully embrace this truth about ourselves, we will remain ambivalent about our true nature [there was division in the crowd]. [44.] Due to this ambivalence, we may be tempted to restrain [arrest] our thinking in terms of our Christ connection, choosing instead to doubt our divine genogram [no one laid hands on him].

[45.] Our religious biases [temple police] are the products of myopic religious thoughts [chief priests and Pharisees], which characterize a limited spiritual perspective. It is these toxic thoughts which contribute to our penchant for denying [arresting] our divine dowry. [46.] Despite our anthropomorphic, God-in-the-sky piety [police/guards] we sense, at a deep soul level, that a literal perspective of sacred scripture and the face value

---
[b] *This process, quantumly speaking, is referred to as cosmic inflation.*

of a material universe lack the depth we need to fully comprehend our true nature. [47.] However, there is still that rigid, deistic part of us [our pharisaical side] that believes we are being deceived by higher thought channels which operate outside of the ego's radar. [48.] We must understand that encrusted belief systems [pharisaical authorities/rulers] are difficult sentiments to recast. [49.] It is from this tunneled 'letter of the law' perspective that we miss higher truths, and distrust [are cursed] any insights which give the appearance of arcane thinking.

[50.] However, as we continue to unfold, this pharisaical glitch in our nature becomes more and more receptive [our Nichodemus openness] to our innate Christ potential [the Jesus of us]. [51.] As this receptivity quickens, we may question our canonical rigidity, wondering how we might be deepened by an expanded spiritual perspective. [52.] Until we move beyond a 'letter of the law' religiosity and a worship of materiality, we will fail to see that the same spirited receptivity that characterizes our super-conscious is the same spirited receptivity that underwrites our subconscious [Galilee]. Until we make that connection, we will continue to assume that no amount of insight [prophet] will produce anything greater in respect to a supposed Higher Self, than what we already believe to be true of us at the sensory level.

Chapter Eight

The Hypocrisy Associated With Unspiritualized Thoughts[a]

[(53)] When we faithfully raise our awareness to a Christed orbit [are dutiful to the Jesus of us], [1.] we come to that higher octave in consciousness where love and wisdom are united [the Mount of Olives]. [2.] From this heightened awareness [early in the morning], our whole consciousness [temple]

---
[a] *The earliest manuscripts do not include John 7:53-8:11.*

is permeated [taught] with a divine essence which influences our entire thought universe [all the people]. ³·If we are not careful, we may allow ourselves to be influenced by encrusted religious beliefs [our scribal and pharisaical bents] which are out of touch with our intuitive nature [women]. From this warped pharisaical perspective, we may automatically condemn an unspiritualized thought [an adulterer] as being useless, instead of discerning its truer, more spiritual value. ⁴·We tend to remember our having had a particular sense-laden, unspiritualized thought [the act of committing adultery] and see it as proof of our mere mortal nature. ⁵·We may even go so far as to stay fixated in a letter-of-the-law mentality [our Moses penchant] by relying on petrified, dogmatic judgment [a stone] to repress any intuitiveness [women] we might feel toward our higher nature.

⁶·It is our own dogmatic tendencies which limit [test] our openness and teachability. Nevertheless, our Christ potential [the Jesus of us] permeates [bends down] every fiber of our being, bathing our consciousness [ground] with Its presiding tactility [writes in the sand]. ⁷·Depending on our degree of enlightenment, we may miss [they questioned him] the nuances of Spirit. And until we have cleansed our consciousness of error [are without sin], we usually find it difficult to refrain from harsh dogmatic judgments [a stone] when it comes to our visceral guidance [women]. ⁸·As was mentioned previously, our Christ potential fills [bends down] our consciousness [ground] with its high voltage presence. ⁹When Spirit moves, its powerful vibration dissolves even the oldest, most encrusted beliefs, assumptions, and prejudices [the elders left first] causing them to lose their resonance and fade away [Jesus was left alone with the woman]. ¹⁰·When we allow that 'still small voice' to guide us [(the Christ as) Jesus spoke], we become aware that we truly have dominion over

any and all negativity [we are not condemned]. [11.] We can state emphatically, through affirmations and denials, that nothing can separate us from our good. Once we become consciously one with the Christ Presence within us, we have the power to transcend any and all error [sin].

A Theological 'San Andreas Fault'

[12.] When we devote ourselves to a living Christmology (thinking, choosing, and acting as expressions of the Cosmic Christ), we bathe our consciousness [world] in the wisdom [light] of that connection. If we attain that high orbit of awareness, the illusion of our not being divine [walking in darkness] will no longer be part of our consciousness. Our wisdom-bathed illumination [light] grounds us in our eternal spiritual beingness [life]. [13.] On the other hand, if we stay stuck in a consciousness characterized by over-amplified dogma [pharisaical thinking], we will fail to recognize or appreciate our true nature. [14.] Despite our having a tremendous dowry of Christ potential [the Jesus of us], the denial of our innate divinity is a gigantic flaw, a theological 'San Andreas Fault' in our consciousness. [15.] Our ego-attached intellect cannot comprehend the real us. [16.] Fortunately, our ability to discern [judge] Truth from error is possible because we are one with the Eternal Isness [the Father] as human embodiments of the Cosmic Christ. [17.] Our mortal mind, however, sees only the cause and effect [testimony of the two witnesses] of duality. [18.] When we are consciously one with our divine nature, we realize that the Eternal Isness [the Father] expresses Itself [testifies] in every level of our being. [19.] If we continue to deny our divinity [do not know the whereabouts of the One (the Father)], we will remain oblivious to our true nature. [20.] Unless and until we master the thought deposits and withdrawals in our waking consciousness [the treasury], the effects on our entire consciousness [temple] will be telling indeed. If, in our waking consciousness, we are unaware of or neglect to work toward our Christhood [his hour had not come], we will experience many *growth fissures* during our spiritual unfoldment.

Orphaning Ourselves From Our Divinity

21. As long as we peripheralize our divinity [I am going away], our quest for discovering who we really are [you will search for me (the Cosmic Christ)] will fail, because of the obstinate denial [we will die] of our falling short [sinned] of our Divine Connection (the recognition that we are Christ expressing as us). 22. The conclusions we draw from an ego-soaked, materially-burdened personality [our unenlightened Jewishness] usually take the form of what could be described as a sort of *theological burlesque,* which seeks to imitate high spiritual principles from a truncated dogmatic perspective.

23. If we continue to orphan ourselves from our innate divinity [operate from below/are of this world], we will fail to appreciate our Christ Individuality [operate from above/are not of this world]. 24. What was shared in the previous verse is so important it must be shared again: if we continue to deny our divinity, we will fall short of the Divine Perfection we seek [we will die in our sins]. We must come into the awareness that we are the Christ expressing *as* us in human form.

25. Our continued denial of our innate divinity is its own indictment. 26. There is a higher order of Being within us [I have much to say in judgment], and that Being (the Cosmic Christ) vivifies and electrifies our divine potential (the Jesus of us) so that It's Christed Vibration [is declared/heard] permeates every meridian and molecule of our consciousness [world].

27. It is not surprising that our sense-addicted ego fails to comprehend the Source [Father] of our divinity. 28. When we are clear about the difference between Truth and error, the Real and the unreal (the process of discernment symbolized by the ['Son of Man']), we will know that our Christ potential comes from the Cosmic Christ (the Formative Aspect of the Eternal Isness) which underwrites all physical existence [we can do nothing on our own]. The Cosmic Christ (the Word) is the Eternal Isness [the Father] expressing Itself as matter [that which is being instructed or taught]. 29. At the risk of repeating this Great Truth, suffice it to say, the Eternal Isness [the One who sent me] is *indivisiblized* (enfleshed in human consciousness) as the Cosmic Christ expressing Itself as the Ominactivity of the One (the Holy Spirit, the Comforter, the Absolute in physicality). 30. Once we understand that, there will be such a shift in awareness that we will experience an incredible sense of wholeness and completion.

Thwarting the Expression of Our Christ Potential

31. When we begin to move beyond the ego-limitations associated with a sense-attached personality [the Jews who believed him], we find ourselves filling our consciousness with spiritual thoughts and inclinations [disciples]. 32. Eventually, we will discover that we are Christ [the Truth] expressing *as* us, which means we can transcend any and all human limitations [be set free].

33. Our sense-soaked thoughts are the products [descendents] of a consciousness rooted in an elementary appreciation of how unlimited our spiritual ideas are [our evolving Abrahamic perspective]. From this rudimentary perspective, we usually do not realize we are enslaved by an error-prone belief system (Adamic consciousness).

34. Unfortunately, when we thwart the expression of our Christ potential [the illumined Jesus of us] by choosing error [sin] over Truth, we enslave ourselves to the consequences of error [sin]. 35. The good news is an ego-induced thought [a slave] is temporal [has no permanent place] in a consciousness which is becoming filled with spiritual thoughts [the family/household]. A spiritually-oriented thought [a son] is divinely inspired [has a place forever]. 36. It is the Christ [Son] embodied *as* us which raises our soul vibration [sets us free]. 37. As long as we choose mortal thoughts [are ready to kill] over Christed thoughts, we will fill our consciousness with an abundance of sense-contaminated thoughts (fledging Abrahamic perspective limited by basic immaturities) which are the result of our settling for material answers to spiritual questions. 38. It would make much more sense for us to seek the answers within (go to the Indwelling Christ [the Father's Presence]) instead of depending on external 'proofs' which satisfy a sense-addicted ego [father].

39. Until we raise our awareness above the fog of duality and separation, we will continue to see ourselves as the products of our cumulative biases and preferences (our gestating Abrahamic perspective is as yet unquickened). As we mature in our thinking, we discover our ideas originate from a more divine connection characterized by a preponderance of Christed thoughts and inclinations [our fully mature Abrahamic nature]. 40. Unfortunately, until we outgrow our desire to worship sense-attachments [try to kill (deny) our divinity], we will miss the point of our human existence.

41. Following the dictates of our ego [our father] keeps us confused and out of sync [illegitimate] with our Christ Self, which is our God Nature [the Father].

42. Until we 'get' that we are Christ expressing *as* us, we will

neglect to honor our Christ potential. [43] Moreover, our worldly appetites will keep us from hearing the 'still small voice.' [44] It is worth repeating that as long as we allow ourselves to be influenced by a sense-corrupted ego [the devil], one which denies our divine nature, we will build a consciousness based on the negation of our true nature [one based on lies]. The thoughts [native language] produced by a sense-soaked ego deny [murder] the expression of any spiritual thoughts [do not stand in the truth], preferring mortal appetites to spiritual attunement. [45] The ego, with its knothole perspective, is unable to comprehend even a brief intermezzi of enlightenment. [46] Clearly, it is difficult, if not impossible, for darkness (the unawareness of our innate divinity) to comprehend the light (the truth of who we really are). [47] A consciousness grounded in Truth is able to grasp [hear] higher truths. On the other hand, a consciousness defined by egocentric chatter is limited by its own centripetal perspective.

[48] In our quest for enlightenment, there may be times when we vacillate between Truth and error [our Samaritan penchant] because our sense-laden personality [Jews who are judgmental] sees everything from an error [demon-possessed] perspective.

[49] The truth is we are Christ at the point of us [not possessed by a demon]. When we have Christed thoughts, we demonstrate our oneness with Spirit [honor the Father]. When we allow error thoughts to dominate our thinking, we reinforce the illusion of separation and duality [dishonor the Father].

[50] When we are true to our God nature, the enlightenment [glory] we seek will come from an interior knowing and connection with the Indwelling Christ [the Judge] which seeks to express Itself more fully *as* us. [51] The truth is when we raise our awareness to the Christ Standard [keep the word] we shall

attain Christhood (eternal life) and move beyond any and all limitations associated with the particular incarnation in which we find ourselves [shall not die].

⁵². As long as we continue to cultivate a sense-veneered, religiously myopic perspective [our tunnel-visioned Jewish nature], we will defend our error [demon-possessed] orientation. Such a sense-limited perspective cannot fathom the limitlessness of a higher order of consciousness. It is too attached to the limited parameters associated with our evolving, and as yet immature, mortal consciousness [our Abrahamic capacity], which places too much emphasis on egocentric thoughts [prophets], which by their very nature are temporal [die]. ⁵³. If we stay stuck in sense-sludge, we will not see that our ability to manifest and create comes from the Christ Mind which expresses Itself through our evolving faith center [Abraham].

⁵⁴. We must move beyond an intellectual perception of God [the Father] which anthropomorphizes God as an entity separate from us, 'out there,' and declare our *indivisible* oneness with the Absolute. ⁵⁵. The mortal mind cannot comprehend that *indivisible* connection. But our super-conscious mind knows we are the Christ at the point of us. ⁵⁶. When our faith [our mature Abrahamic ability] is elevated to the level of pure knowing, we will see that we have the capacity to turn our Christ potential into fully-demonstrated Christhood [see my day].

⁵⁷. As long as we depend only on our five senses [fifty years], we will see the world through the filter of our Adamic consciousness [our worldly Jewishness]. We will question our connection to the eternality of Spirit. ⁵⁸. It will take the formative power of faith [our Abrahamness] to help us move beyond sense entrapments.

⁵⁹. The knowledge of our *indivisibleness* with the Eternal Isness (God, the One Reality, the Absolute) takes a leap in faith. Unfortunately the hard, rigid,

materialistic beliefs and biases [stones] produced by a recalcitrant ego will never bring us the clarity we need [Jesus hid Himself]. A material consciousness [the temple grounds] is not the kind of *soil* which brings enlightenment.

Chapter Nine

Horizontally Slanted and Vertically Challenged

1. So often, when we re-enter the human experience we fail to remember who we really are [we are blind from birth].[a]

2. Although we re-embody with our higher spiritual faculties [disciples] intact at a super-conscious level of awareness, we tend to forget we are spiritual beings having another human experience. We sense there is that within us, a superior inner knowledge [Rabbi], which 'documents' who we are, but we fail to see the causal relationship between our current error thinking [sins] and our previous incarnational baggage [parents].

3. Although reincarnational experiences are not necessary conditions for enlightenment [neither man nor parents sinned (missed the mark)], we have opportunities in each re-embodiment to discover our innate divinity and unfold into our Christhood [reveal/display God's works]. 4. Each successive incarnation requires that we remain open to our divine heirship [day], or the reincarnational experience [night (numbing)] itself will make it difficult for us to see the light (the truth of our innate divinity). 5. However, we can be sure that during each physical embodiment, the Christ Presence [the I Am of us] permeates our consciousness [the world]. It is the Christ Presence [our I Am-ness] which illumi-

---

[a] The self of us which remembers our past lives and concurrent lives in other dimensions of being is our Quantum Self, the composite of all of our human and intradimensional incarnations.

nates [lights] our consciousness [the world].

6. We can remove blocks to our higher understanding by calling on our Higher Nature. We do this by recognizing the transparency and malleability of the physical universe [forming mud with spittle] to gain the clarity we need [saliva placed on eyes] to remember our spiritual origins. 7. It is this recognition of the interplay between Spirit and matter that propels us toward the understanding [sends us to the Pool of Siloam/Shiloha] that the material universe is an illusion [he came home able to see] we have created to sustain us while we grapple with the deeper, more cosmic (spiritual) dimensions of our being.

8. The illusion is perpetuated by our sense thoughts [neighbors] which characterize a consciousness that feels inadequate [begs] when it comes to understanding the greater mysteries of life. 9. If we remain attached to materiality we will vacillate between seeing ourselves as merely flesh and blood human beings on the one hand, and suspect we are more than human on the other. However, in the depths of our soul we know that our human-ness is really a dense vibration of our spiritual eternality.

10. We may wonder how we, as infinite beings having a finite human experience, can gain the clarity we need [eyes opened] to understand the infinite. 11. If we give ourselves a moment to consider our true worth, we will see that we are the ones who block our understanding. We need only grasp the truth that we are beings who have opportunities to actualize our Christ potential [the Jesus of us]. We are Spirit as matter. We are infinite beings who choose finite experiences. We must give ourselves permission to see matter for what it is – frozen thought. It is that kind of clarity [going to the Pool of Siloam] which will bring us enlightenment.

12. Until we reach that level of awareness, we will not ap-

preciate the extent of our spiritual capabilities. [13.] There is that part of us, our pharisaical nature, which refuses to see us as elevated beings, and distrusts anything resembling higher thought. [14.] The truth is, whenever we distance ourselves from material thoughts and concerns [a Sabbath experience], it is at that very moment we can gain the clarity we need [have our eyes opened] to see the quantum interplay between Spirit and matter.

[15.] We must move beyond dogmatic footprints [our pharisaical bent] to understand the veiled divinity in matter [mud formed from spittle]. [16.] Giving undue attention to the literality of religious texts, as well as to the temporality of physical form [our pharisaical nature], prevents us from going inside [a Sabbath experience] to gain the clarity we need. However, there is that within us which questions our allegiance to the sterility of external forms and the empty formulas associated with religious rhetoric. We may even wonder how spiritual insights [miraculous signs] can come from a consciousness characterized by spiritual inertia [sin].

[17.] As we struggle to comprehend what appears to be a Spirit as matter dichotomy [turning again to the sighted blind man], we wonder if we can gain insights which will help us connect with our inner guidance [prophet]. [18.] In our refusal to truly be open to new teachings [our Jewish penchant], we will find it difficult to nullify any of the limitations and warped perspectives [parents] that characterize our sense consciousness. [19.] A chronic focus on materiality keeps us vertically challenged – that is to say, we remain unable to comprehend the truth that we can rise above our spiritual inertia [blindness] and actualize our latent divinity.

[20.] As we continue to question old beliefs, we will come to the realization that each newly formed insight [son] is the product of our previous thinking [parents]. But we also know we can elevate our awareness and catch glimpses of truth, even though we may be chronically attached to sense appetites [are born blind]. [21.] From our old, sense-veneered perspectives, we are clueless as to how spirited ideas originate, particularly since they seem so uncharacteristic of our normal thinking. Our usual tact is to show perfunctory interest in the merits of a newly-formed spiritual insight [let it speak for itself].

[22.] For most of us, the difficulty in accepting transformational changes is that they challenge our old way of thinking [parents], and particularly our religious biases [our Jewish proclivities]. Given that myopic perspective, we are prone to disavow any thoughts or inclinations which hint of any possibility that we are beings with Christ potential [the Jesus of us], let alone our *indivisible* connection with the Cosmic Christ expressing Itself as us. We generally keep those Christed thoughts out of a spiritually quarantined consciousness [synagogue]. [23.] Until we have fully embraced our divine nature, we tend to let newly formed, spiritually-charged ideas fend for themselves in a spiritually anorexic consciousness.

[24.] Steeped in duality [a second summons], we find it difficult to accept our divine status [we sin (remain materialistically-focused)]. [25] In our quickening consciousness we are tempted to place spirituality above religiosity because spirituality, we sense, may give us the clarity we seek. We make that assumption because we have felt Spirit's inviolate impulses (we have become sighted) from time to time. [26.] Unfortunately, our egocentric sense consciousness is incapable of grafting hidden truths successfully onto Adamic branches. [27.] The ego's inability to plummet spiritual depths keeps it unbalanced and unreceptive to divine guidance.

[28.] It is this recalcitrant nature of the ego which prompts us to deny [hurl insults/revile] our divinity. If we choose to be ego-enslaved, all we can see is that our evolutionarily-stamped identity [our Mosesic development] is the only basis of our existence. [29.] The ego has no qualms accepting evolution over involution and matter over Spirit.

[30.] What is remarkable is how the ego remains oblivious to the connectivity between Spirit and matter. [31.] At the level of Spirit, there is no error [sin]. And because we are Spirit expressing Itself *as* matter, we can transcend error at the human level if we choose to embrace that Truth. [32.] A consciousness which is steeped in materiality blocks its own ability to comprehend esoteric truths. And so each new thought which is the product of that warped awareness reinforces our denial [is born blind] of our innate divinity. [33.] However, because we are divine at our core, we can master our human vulnerabilities (overcome the world) by moving from horizontal thinking (coma consciousness) to vertical thinking (a Christed outlook).

[34.] Unfortunately, it is the nature of a sense-addicted ego to discount our divine origins. Any thought or inclination toward our divine connection is summarily dismissed.

[35.] However, because of our potentializing Christ unfoldment [the illumined Jesus of us], we have the ability to draw distinctions between what is true and what is false, what serves our highest good and what curbs our highest good. [36.] As we become more aware of our divine connection we may experience periods of ambivalence as we discern what is true and what is false. [37.] Rest assured, however, anytime we see things from a higher, more altruistic perspective, we are listening to the 'still small voice.'

[38.] We need only trust our inner guidance and affirm [worship] our oneness with Spirit. [39.] By its very nature, our Christ potential [the Jesus of us] equips our consciousness [the world] with the powers of discernment and discrimination [judgment] to see rightly. When we seek truth, even though we initially fail to see [are blind] our divine connection, we will gain the clarity we need to fully demonstrate our divinity. On the other hand, when we peripheralize (deny) our divinity [remain attached to materiality], we remain oblivious [blind] to the spiritual principles that can set us free from the gravitational pull of error.

40. Until we gain this clarity, there is that egocentric part of us, our pharisaical side, which worships the sensory accouterments of religious practice and the material world. It refuses to leave its hedonic perch (our Adamistic penchant), favoring materiality over spirituality.

41. If we are unaware [are blind] of our innate divinity, we are not consciously complicit [guilty] in failing to demonstrate that divinity. However, when we are reasonably aware of our divine status and choose sense-coated appetites over spiritual aspirations [claim to see], our intentional culpability [guilt] slows our lack of spiritual progress. It seems as if our material attachments (horizontal slants) keep us vertically (spiritually) challenged.

Chapter Ten

We Are Shepherded by Our I Am Connection

1. It is a perennial esoteric teaching that if our human personality [man] is not the product of [does not enter] a Christed belief system [sheep pen/sheep fold] which is the out-picturing of our Christ Connection [gate], we tend to allow a cattle drive of materialistic thoughts [thieves and robbers] to form outposts in our consciousness. 2. When our human personality [man] is in alignment with its Christ Connection [gate], our thoughts [sheep] are the products of our

Christed awareness [Shepherd]. 3. Our spiritually-attuned will [porter/gatekeeper/watchman] ignites our receptivity to our divine connection [opens the gate], making it possible for our thoughts [sheep] to resonate at their higher spiritual essences [hear the (still small) voice]. Our willingness [gatekeeper/porter/watchman] to raise our thoughts [call the sheep] to their higher spiritual essences [name] grounds us in Spirit. 4. A consciousness filled with Christed thoughts [all are brought out] is the result of a highly attuned spiritual will which directs our thoughts [sheep] and actions [goes ahead of them]. From this heightened awareness, our thoughts [sheep] align with our spiritual I Amness (the still small voice). 5. When we reach this level of unfoldment, our thoughts are attuned with Spirit and not the ego [stranger]. In fact, our spirit-filled thoughts invariably operate at a higher obit than the earth-bound thoughts coming from the ego [stranger]. 6. As we begin to actualize our Christ potential [the Jesus of us], we are less deterred by a materially-focused ego.

7. It must be remembered that spiritually-charged thoughts [sheep] come from our Christ Connection [gate]. 8. Before we come to this heightened awareness, our consciousness tends to be filled with materialistic thoughts [thieves and robbers]. However, spiritually-quickened thoughts [sheep] can transform even the most materialistic thoughts into their higher inviolate essences. 9. The Christ *as* us is the Sacred Connection [gate] through which our materialistic thoughts give way to spiritual aspirations [salvation], creating a spiritually-attuned consciousness [pasture]. 10. Materialistic thoughts represent a consciousness which tries to circumvent [steal] our divine heirship by denying [killing/destroying] any thoughts which lead to spiritual insights. On the other hand, the embodied Cosmic Christ, by Its very presence,

guarantees that we have ready access to the fullness of Spirit [eternal life].

11. The Good Shepherd (Eternal Isness, God, the Infinite Invisibleness, the One Reality) embodies Itself in human form [lays down its life] to raise our thoughts [sheep] to their highest spiritual essences. 12. Our human personality [hired hand] is not the Self [Shepherd] from which our spiritual ideas [sheep] come. When our human personality is defined by materialistic thoughts and inclinations [wolves], we tend to ignore [abandon] spiritual inclinations. It is not surprising that from this sense-soaked materialistic consciousness, we allow a worldly belief system [wolf] to dominate our thinking. 13. A sense-dependent human personality [hired hand] has a difficult time honoring its higher spiritual nature.

14. Because we are the Eternal Isness, the One Reality [Shepherd], expressing Itself *as* us, the thoughts [sheep] we hold in mind will produce similar thoughts [sheep] after their kind [the sheep know me]. 15. As the Only Begotten Son of the Eternal Isness [Father], the Cosmic Christ embodies Itself [lays down Its life] so that no spiritually-quickened thought [sheep] remains unexpressed. 16. Unquickened thoughts [other sheep], which spring from the limited egocentric perspective of human consciousness [are not of this sheep pen], will be transformed into their highest spiritual essences [listen to my voice] when all of our thoughts [flock] align with our Spiritual I Am [Shepherd].

17. It is the Cosmic Christ, the formative aspect of the Eternal Isness, the One Reality [Father], which makes it possible for us to return to (remember) our true nature. 18. There is no other way [no one takes it from me] for us to be transformed from our limited human awareness into an expanded spiritual awareness, except through the out-working of the Christ Principle [I lay it down/I have the

power to lay it down], which is the formative aspect [the command received] of the Eternal Isness, the Infinite Invisibleness [Father].

[19.] If we choose to remain the products of religious biases and dogmatic preoccupations [our unillumined Jewish penchants] instead of the benefactors of spiritual aspirations, we will tend to be exclusive [divided] in our religious beliefs and treat others who hold different views as outsiders. [20.] From this purely egocentric perch, we allow our error thoughts to rule [are demon-possessed] and miss hearing the "still small voice." [21.] On the other hand, we can move beyond the superficiality of a letter-of-the-law mentality and see the hidden wisdom contained in a Spirit-of-the-law approach.

Christed Actions Come From a Christed Consciousness

[22.] When we are in a peaceful, reverential state of awareness [Jerusalem], there is no hesitation to sacrifice lower, more sense-coated thoughts for higher, more spiritually-charged thoughts [a feast/Festival of Dedication experience] on the 'altar' of a Christ-centered consciousness. This is particularly important if we have allowed our higher spiritual faculties to remain dormant [winter]. [23.] Our Christ-aware consciousness [temple] is the localized field which houses our Christ potential [the Jesus of us]. In this state of heightened awareness, our thoughts are coated [walking under the portico/colonnade] with wisdom and love [Solomon's Temple]. [24.] Unless we move past our religious biases and ritualized forms of limited understanding [our worldly Jewish orientation], we will find it difficult to accept our divine heirship [the presence of the Indwelling Christ].

[25.] What happens is that we invariably receive spiritual insights [miracles], which are by nature [name] emanations from the Eternal Isness, the Absolute [Father], [26.] but we discount them [do not believe] because we are radiating at a lower level of awareness [are not my sheep]. [27.] Thoughts which are Christed [sheep listening to the inner voice] produce similar Christed thoughts [follow me]. [28.] As has been mentioned before, Christed thoughts come from a Christed Consciousness [eternal life] and remain the instruments of divinely ordered actions (firmly held in one's hand).

[29.] Our entire mental universe of Christed thoughts comes from the Eternal Isness, the Infinite Invisibleness [Father] which is the Source of our good. God (the Eternal Isness, the One Reality) expressing as the Cosmic Christ, is the First Cause of all divinely ordered movement [firmly held in my Father's hand]. [30.] Our connection to this divinely ordered universe is this: we are the Eternal Isness, the One Reality [Father] expressing Itself as the Christ at the point of us.

[31.] All of this being said, if we remain caught up in religiously myopic beliefs and attitudes [our unenlightened Jewishness], we will fill our consciousness with rigid thoughts and biases [stones] to justify fossilized religious habits [throwing stones]. [32.] Because we are filled with so much Christ potential [the Jesus of us], our consciousness is flooded with higher spiritual insights [miracles] which spring from our God Nature (Eternal Isness [Father]). Unfortunately, rigid materialistic thoughts [stones] which are the products of a recalcitrant ego surface from time-to-time, and chorus a prejudiced error perspective against any thoughts which allude to our divinity.

[33.] What is particularly troublesome for a sense-addicted ego is not necessarily our spiritual insights, but their internal source of origin. If we remain a product of an ego-driven human personality, we will find it difficult to comprehend that we are God expressing *as* us. If we remain influenced by an error-oriented ego, we consider any thought of our divine heirship as disrespectful [blasphemous] of the ego's sovereignty. [34.] However, the truth is, the nature of physicality [that which is written] is based on the cosmic principle [law] that consciousness, not matter, is the ground of all being. Therefore, as super-conscious spiritual beings [gods, God desires gods] in pre-human form, we created the material universe. [35.] As embodied super-conscious expressions [gods] of the Cosmic Christ [the word of God], we are *indivisible* composites [unbroken scripture] of the One Consciousness. [36.] Imagine how powerful and pervasive the *indivisibility* must be between the Cosmic Christ [the One whom the Father (God) set apart] and the Father [God] at both a macro-consciousness level and at a human consciousness [world] level! Unfortunately, it is the nature of an insolent ego to trivialize [blaspheme] the truth that we are the Christ [God's Son] enfleshed *as* us.

[37.] Christed actions come from a Christed Consciousness, which is God's Consciousness ideating in human form. [38] Such a highly attuned consciousness must evolve past a worldly ego which finds our divine heirship difficult to comprehend. [39.] If we choose to remain stuck in an egocentric bubble, we will try unsuccessfully to quantify [seize] the unquantifiable as we float in an air of illusion.

[40.] Eventually we get to the place where our actualized Christ potential [the Jesus of us] permeates our stream of thoughts [Jordan] and quickens the intellect [our John quality], cleansing it [baptizing it] of its error orientation. [41.] Our ego-driven intellect (our unenlightened John quality), no matter how superior it may be, will never be able to fully comprehend the nuances of spiritually-charged insights [miraculous signs] and extrasensory capacities. Ultimately, a quickened intellect [our illumined John quality] will sense the need for an interior transformation (baptism).

42. When that interior cleansing (baptism) takes place, all of our thoughts and inclinations will be in alignment [many believed] with our Christ potential.

Chapter Eleven

Our Lazarus Legacy

1. Oftentimes, when we seek to rise above human challenges [go to Bethany], we forget that deep within us is a revitalizing power center fueled by our Christ potential. When we allow this spiritual vitality to remain dormant and untapped [a Lazarus experience], our inclination toward service devoted to others [our Martha proclivity] and our desire to understand spiritual truths [our Mary aspirations] are compromised. 2. Because of our devotion to the truth [our Mary aspect] and our willingness to offer Spirit our best [pouring perfume], we will gain the understanding [feet] we need and enjoy an increase in vitality [hair], if we remind ourselves of the untapped potential within us [our Lazarus latency]. 3. It is important to remember that our love for the Truth and our devotion to serving others [sisters] will lose their savor if we forget [are sick/ill] our divine roots.

4. Spiritual lethargy [sickness], in spite of its energy leakage, cannot separate us from Spirit [end in death], but its dormancy is a reminder that we come pre-wired with explosive divine power [God's glory] which can be harnessed [glorified] through the Indwelling Christ [God's Son].

5. Our actualized Christ potential [the Jesus of us] underwrites our devotion to service [our Marthaness] and our love for the Truth [our Mary expression], even if we allow it to remain untapped [our Lazarus tendency]. 6. Despite its neglect, our Christ potential (the Jesus of us) remains the foundation of our physical and spiritual [two days] health.

7. We can begin to tap into our Christ potential when we fill our conscious awareness with Christed thoughts [go to Judea]. 8 What happens early in our unfoldment is that although we may be influenced by an extraordinarily powerful spiritual insight [a Rabbi], our religious biases [our rigid Jewishness] generally foster calcified, dogmatic postures [stones] that limit our expanded awareness.

9. What we must remember is that to complete our soul work (aligning our human self with our Christ Self), we need to develop all of our core spiritual qualities [twelve hours (twelve disciples)]. That soulfulness comes from one place – inner clarity [daylight]. When we follow our interior guidance by listening to the 'still small voice' [walk by day], we will not stumble. 10. On the other hand, when we follow the dictates of an unhealthy ego [walk by night], we generally remain oblivious [stumble] to our inner guidance, and consequently fall out of trajectory with our enlightenment.

11. Regardless of how long we have neglected to acknowledge our innate divinity [our Lazarus susceptibility], our Christ potential is always present. 12. As long as our spiritual abilities [disciples] remain unquickened, we will fail to see the consequences of our error proneness [sleep]. 13. However, from a soul growth perspective, the chronic denial of our divinity [death] is much more debilitating than merely neglecting [sleeping naturally] our spiritual growth.

14. Even if mindless neglect [our Lazarus vulnerability] of our untapped Christ potential turns into outright denial [Lazarus is dead], 15. because we shut down all avenues of spiritual understanding [I was not there], our Christ potential remains firmly planted in our being.

16. At this phase of our developing awareness, our attempt to understand the nuances of our spiritual growth [the Thomas/Didymus phase of our growth] is defined by our dependence on

the material world for answers [let us die with him].

[17] Despite the presence of our innate Christ potential [the Jesus of us], we may allow outer appearances to dim our spiritual vitality [a Lazarus experience]. Be assured, however, that this dormant vitality lies in the vitalizing power center [tomb] deep within us. Nothing is lost in Spirit. The foundation (represented by the number four) of our evolving Christhood is firmly set within us. [18] Our ability to rise above human limitations of any kind [go to Bethany] and attune our spiritual and human states of being (represented by the number two) is possible when we remain cognizant of the abiding peace and harmony [Jerusalem] which are our birthrights. [19] Even if we remain influenced by worldly forms and appearances [our rigid Jewishness], we can still find comfort in our devoted service [our Martha expression] to humankind and in our love for the Truth [our Mary expression], even if it is from a limited religious perspective [brother].

[20] As we begin to sense a deeper connection with Spirit [hear Jesus coming], we generally react in two distinct ways. We either step up our willingness to serve [our Martha response] by going without (serving others), or express our love for hidden truths [our Mary response] by going within [home].

[21] Sometimes we get so caught up in our devotion to service [our Martha penchant] that we neglect to charge our spiritual batteries [brother dies]. [22] However, despite our focus on outer forms of spiritual growth, we have a growing sense in the inviolate omnipresence of Spirit [God, (the One Reality, the Absolute)].

[23] Because we are Christs potentializing [the Jesus of us], our spiritual nature [brother] permeates our consciousness and underwrites our ability to re-discover [rise again] our innate divinity.

24. If we are not careful, we may allow our devotion to serving others [our Martha influence] to become a substitute for the inner work we need to raise our consciousness to a Christed orbit [a resurrection experience]. Our spiritual growth requires both disciplined introspection and Christed actions.

25. Because we are Christs potentializing [our Jesusness], we have the ability to raise our consciousness to its super-conscious level [a resurrection experience] and achieve conscious oneness with the Absolute [life (eternal life)]. When we reach that level of awareness [live], our human personality is transformed [dies] into its higher spiritual essence. 26. And when we maintain that level of heightened awareness [live and believe in me], we transcend ego limitations and remain at a Christed level of thinking, feeling, and being [never die].

27. Once we come to the realization that the same Christ that expressed Itself as Jesus is the same Christ that expresses Itself *as* us, we intuit that the Christ embodied *as* us is the same Universal Cosmic Christ [Son of God] which underwrites the material (visible) universe.

28. When our 'service to others self' [our Martha expression] integrates with our 'love for the Truth self' [our Mary expression], we are in a strong position to actualize the inner guidance we receive from Spirit [Teacher]. 29. Our love for the Truth [our Mary quality] always readies us to express our inner light.

30. Even though we may not have fully adopted the higher teachings into our belief system [the place where Martha met him], we are preparing our consciousness [village] for a fuller understanding of our Christ Nature. 31. It will take some time for our worldly, but awakening inclinations [Jews], to be raised to their higher spiritual essences.

32. Our search for the Truth [our Mary expression] usually takes us on a collision course

with an existing belief system [the place where Jesus met Martha]. It is at this intersection of the old meeting the new that we must seek greater understanding [she knelt/fell at his feet]. Without it, we will fall into the ego trap of giving into outer appearances, because we've neglected to keep our spiritual batteries charged [brother who dies].

33. If we are conscientious in our unfoldment, we will find that our love for the Truth cleanses [weeps] our consciousness of error, and works toward purging [weeping] our worldly thoughts and religious biases [our Adamic Jewishness] of their materialistic tendencies.

34. The question we must ask ourselves is – to what extent have we neglected our Christ potential [where have you laid him]? The answer lies in our willingness to open ourselves up to Spirit. 35. When our openness is genuine, our Christ potential can be released [Jesus wept].

36. Our worldly orientations [our Jewish bent] begin to lose their temporal influence as they drift toward their higher essences. This brings an inner harmonics [love] and vitality to our evolving awareness.

37. We may ask ourselves at this juncture of our development why we allow our spiritual vitality to remain dormant [our Lazarus state of consciousness], when the Christ Presence permeates [opens] every aspect of our consciousness, including our subconsciousness [eyes of the blind].

38. The answer is our Christ potential [our Jesusness] has Its residency in the vitalizing power center deep within us, called the 'still point' [tomb]. However, we block access to the 'still point' [cave/tomb] with a rigid belief [stone] in our separation from Spirit.

39. If we want to fully express our Christhood, we must roll away the 'stone' of the illusion of any distance between us and the Eternal Isness (the One Reality, the Absolute). We must

accept the presence of the Eternal Isness in all of Its divine aspects [Divine Mind, Cosmic Christ, Holy Spirit]. We must not think all is lost, no matter how much we neglect [there is a bad odor] our divine heirship – spiritually, mentally, emotionally, or physically [four days].

40. We must remain open and receptive to the truth of our innate divinity in order to actualize our Christ Consciousness [see the glory of God].

41. We have the wherewithal to remove the 'stone' of denial and illusion of our separation from the Eternal Isness (God, the One Reality). We need only affirm our oneness with the Eternal Isness [Father, (God, the Infinite Invisibleness)]. 42. The more we affirm that truth, the higher our thoughts [the people/crowd standing there] will gravitate toward their spiritual essences.

43. Each time we actualize [call forth in a loud voice] our Christ potential [the Jesus of us], we literally bring to life the dormant vital forces [our Lazarus state of consciousness] that are instrumental in raising [come forth] our energies to their Christed vibrations.

44. When we awaken our latent divine potential [the dead man comes out], we will experience a powerful rebirth [represented by the strips of linen] in our service to humankind [linen draped hands] and a greater understanding [linen draped feet] of spiritual laws and principles. This awakening generally begins with intellectual receptivity to the prospects of our enlightenment. However, initially we will be limited to a thin veil of intellectual awakening [cloth/napkin covering face], as we grapple with our divine potential. Eventually, we will have the courage to express our Christ Nature each-consecutive-moment-of-now [are unbound].

The Gyrations of a Materially-Fixated Consciousness

45 Because of our devotion to the truth [our Maryness], most of

our previous dogmatic thinking [our regimented Jewishness] softens. We begin to see the benefits associated with demonstrating our Christ potential [the Jesus of us].

⁴⁶ It will come as no surprise that inner transformation takes time. Until we become fully Christed, we will have thoughts which spring from long-standing beliefs and dogmas [our pharisaical viewpoint] that deny our divinity. ⁴⁷ It is these deeply-rooted beliefs and biases [chief priests and Pharisees] that characterize our worship of outer forms [our Sanhedrinian mindset]. The presence of higher spiritual thoughts and insights [miracles] presents a threat to a materially-focused ego. ⁴⁸· The transformation of our body, mind, and soul [everyone] is possible when we conscientiously unfold toward our Christhood [let him go on like this]. And yet, it is this inner flowering which troubles us if we are the products of an unenlightened ego. We may be particularly concerned since we know a dominating personal will and rigid intellect [Romans] can become influenced by an inner urge to challenge established biases [take away our place] of a materially-fixated consciousness [nation].

⁴⁹· The longer we remain calcified in cosmetic theology [our Caiaphasic orientation] and unduly influenced by the world of appearances, we will find it difficult, if not impossible, to see the *indivisible* connection between Spirit and matter. ⁵⁰· From the viewpoint of our fossilized ego, it is better to deny any possibility of our Christ potential [let one man die] than allow the thoughts of our divine heirship to supplant a materially-fixated consciousness [nation].

⁵¹· The unenlightened us, which is unaware of our true Self [he did not say this on his own], caters to a worldly ego [high priest] and thrives on the neglect of our innate Christ potential [the Jesus of us]. This neglect includes compromising religious convictions [the Jewish nation] and giving perfunctory

attention to spiritual insights. ⁵². Numbed by our vacillation between spiritually-charged, religious convictions [nation] and a materialistically-driven ego, we tend to discount [scatter] any and all divinely-inspired ideas [the children of God]. ⁵³· If our consciousness is dominated by this level of egocentric awareness [from that day], we are prone to deny our *indivisibleness* with Spirit [plot to take this life].

⁵⁴· When we are not open to the Truth, ego-driven thoughts dominate our thinking, being, and doing [Jesus no longer moves about openly]. As a result, the richness of our divine circuitry [our Ephraimic inheritance], with its innate spiritual capacities [the disciples], is suppressed [withdraws to a desert].

⁵⁵· It takes conscious volition to move from sense consciousness (coma consciousness) to spiritual consciousness [go up to Jerusalem for Passover]. ⁵⁶· Until we commit ourselves to our Truth walks, we will arrest our Christ potential [look/search for Jesus] by keeping It dormant within us. As long as It (our innate Christ potential) remains unused, we will not 'harvest' our untapped spiritual powers [go to the Feast]. ⁵⁷ Given that knothole perspective, blighted by its dogmatic and self-aggrandizing thought patterns [chief priests and Pharisees], it is not surprising that we remain oblivious (arrested) to our true nature.

Chapter Twelve

Our Love For the Truth Bathes Us in Understanding

¹· As we begin to experience a unified consciousness [symbolized by six days], our interior unfoldment takes us from one *cusp of consciousness* to another [a Passover experience]. This inner *wholing* is the result of our becoming more aware of our Christ potential [the Jesus of us]. This conscious heirship makes it possible for us to overcome the perplexities and com-

plexities of sense consciousness [our journey to Bethany]. Restoring, and then re-restoring, the awareness of our divine nature [our Lazarus legacy] seems to be a consistent theme in our human experience.

2. Our whole consciousness is revitalized [a dinner is given] when we honor our Christ potential [the Jesus of us]. The more we apply truth principles in service to others [our Marthaness], the greater our chances will be at restoring and harmonizing latent energies [our Lazarus legacy] to their formative power. 3. When our love for the Truth [our Mary quality] is pure and unrestrained in its simple elegance [a liter/pint of pure nard (nardin)], we can gain such clarity and depth of spiritual understanding [the washing of Jesus' feet] that our entire consciousness [house] will be filled with the harmonics of absolute bliss [fragrance of perfume].

4. However, we must always beware of our penchant for choosing sense appetites [our Judas Iscariotness] over spiritual sustenance. 5. If we are not careful, we will fall into the trap of negating our access to the omnipresence of abundance. Such a warped perspective springs from a sense-prone consciousness which fails to grasp the implications of its materialistically-inclined thought system. 6. Sense appetites [our Judas proclivity] are not satisfied with spent pleasures [the poor]. It is our desire for materiality [the money bag] which steals opportunities for spiritual deepening.

7. On the other hand, we have the innate capacity to achieve conscious oneness with Spirit and enjoy absolute bliss [perfume] when we reach the awakening awareness [day] that our Christ potential [the Jesus of us] will give way to [be buried] the full realization our Christhood. 8. Spent pleasures [the poor] are the products of a sense-hungry egocentric consciousness which is never satisfied with material delights. If we allow ourselves to be defined by a sense-laden ori-

entation, we will fail to grasp our innate wholeness.

The Urge to Resist Recharging Our Spiritual Batteries

9. Many of our established religious beliefs and dogmatic views [a large crowd of Jews] can be tempered with the awareness that we can actualize our Christ potential [the Jesus of us] and restore latent spiritual energies [our Lazarus legacy] when we rediscover our innate divine nature [be raised from the dead]. 10. However, we must not be surprised to find that encrusted dogmatic views and deep-seated religious biases [chief priests] may surface from time-to-time, which resist [kill] any inclination to recharge our spiritual batteries [a Lazarus experience]. 11. The good news is, despite a recalcitrant ego, we will find ourselves turning previously ingrained religious biases [our rigid Jewishness] into their spiritually oriented counterparts once we begin actualizing our Christ potential [the Jesus of us].

Our Blossoming Christ Potential

12. As we awaken [the next day] to our innate divinity, spiritually attuned thoughts [a great crowd] demonstrate our readiness to receive the truths [feast/festival] which are already grafted onto our Christ potential [the Jesus of us]. And the way we access our innate divinity is by going to that place within which connects us with that abiding stillness and peace [Jerusalem].

13. Our spiritually-attuned thoughts [the responsive crowd] are evidence of our resolve to strengthen our faith [spreading palm branches] and deepen our spirituality. When our error states of consciousness are overcome, our entire thought universe is bathed in *thanks-living* [Hosannas]. Wholeness is conferred upon [blessed] our hu-

manness when we realize we are the Christ [Lord] expressing at the point of us. Our wholeness [blessedness] is assured once we attune ourselves with our I-Am-ness [the King of Israel].

14. We must realize that our actualized Christ potential [our Jesusness] elevates us above mere base instincts [donkey], because our very nature [it is written] is divine.

15. Our superior intuition [Daughter of Zion] is the catalyst for our evolving spiritual awareness and growth [your king is coming]. All we have to do is transform our base instincts [donkey's colt] into their higher spiritual equivalents.

16. At this point in our unfoldment, our core-spiritual abilities [disciples] are not fully developed [do not understand]. Once we realize our Christ potential [Jesus is glorified], we will see that our very nature [what has been written about us] is truly divine.

17. Christed thoughts and beliefs [crowd], which are indicative of our becoming more open to our innate divinity, spring from a deep reservoir [tomb] of spiritual awareness within us. They are evidence of a restoration of latent spiritual energies [our Lazarus legacy] which surface whenever we rediscover our innate goodness [being raised from the dead]. 18. When our awareness is raised to a higher spiritual orbit [miraculous sign], many of our worldly thoughts [people] are transformed into their higher spiritual essences. 19. Other, more dogmatic and deep-seated religious biases [our pharisaicalness] will remain embedded in our over-all consciousness [the world] until they, too, are transformed to their higher vibrations.

From Mind Auction to Mind Action

20. It is our highly intellectual nature [the Greek of us] which readies us [goes to worship] to receive inviolate truths [attend the feast]. 21. This intellectual

curiosity [our Greekishness] is the result of an inner fire or force of interior vitality [our Phillipness], which drives our penchant for searching for new intellectual insights [Bethsaida]. It lies dormant in our subconscious [Galilee] until we become aware of our Christ potential. 22. It is this inner vitality [the Phillip of us] which gives us strength [the Andrew of us] and fortifies our mental capacities, turning mind *auction* (worldly appetites) into spirited mind *action* (spiritual aspirations).

23. Because of that readily available Christ potential [the Jesus of us], our awareness is raised [the hour has come] to its super-conscious state [is glorified] so that we are able to clearly discern between Truth and error [the Son of Man has come]. 24 If a higher truth [kernel/grain of wheat] enters our conscious awareness [falls to the ground] and is not applied to transform our consciousness [dies], it simply becomes a spent divine idea [single seed/grain]. But if we allow it to replace older thought patterns which have served their purpose [die], it will generate many divine ideas [seeds/grain] and expand our thinking.

25. If we remain the product of sense consciousness [love this life], we will not receive [lose] the spiritual insights we need to master the art of living. However, when we consistently choose spiritual thoughts over worldly thoughts, we will unfold into our Christ Consciousness [eternal life].

26. When we surrender [serve] to our Christ Nature, we will transform our human consciousness [servant]. We accomplish that by becoming consciously one [honor] with the Eternal Isness, the One Reality, God [Father] which is expressing Itself at the point of us.

Realizing Our Christ Potential or Rationing It

27. We might wonder why we have chosen to incarnate again [our hearts are troubled]. We

may even ask ourselves if it is possible to gain clemency from the karmic baggage we carry from one incarnation to another [be saved from this hour]. But we are here to become the best Christs we can be. [28.] We are here to remind ourselves that we are God [the Father, (the Absolute)] expressing *as* us [glorifying God's nature] through the Christ. When we come to that realization, our entire consciousness vibrates at a higher spiritual essence [a voice came from heaven]. That is because our Christ Nature expresses [glorifies] Itself as us. [29.] Our entire thought universe [crowd] resonates [thunders] with Christed ideas [angels].

[30.] Once we begin to actualize our Christ potential [the Jesus of us], the higher, spiritually-charged vibrations associated with our unfolding Christhood begin to harmonize every aspect of our being. [31.] As this field of inner harmonics expands [passes judgment], our unenlightened ego [the prince], which rules our human personality [the world], becomes subordinate to our evolving Christness. [32.] Our body, mind, and soul [the earth] are harmonized by every thought, word, and action [drawing all men/people] that comes with our evolving perfection. [33.] What is being described above is the process in which the human *self* unfolds into the Christ *Self*.

[34.] Our consciousness may be flooded with a multitude of egocentric thoughts [crowd] which spring from the illusion that we are sinful beings (those who succumb to the illusionary power of outer appearances). If we remain a product of this fractured awareness, we tend to believe we must wait for a divine fiat from an exalted Messianic Being [a Christ] 'out there' in order to be saved. If we are the product of an unenlightened ego, we will have difficulty seeing that we have the ability to raise our awareness to a more sacred height, instead of allowing it to remain flat lined in its egocentric trajectory [the Son of Man must be lifted up].

35. Since we have the power of choice, we can honor our Christ Self [the Light within] or deny [walk in the dark] our innate divinity. 36. If we have the courage and good sense to fully embrace our Christ Nature [the Light], our waking consciousness will be filled with divinely-inspired ideas [sons of light]. It is for us to choose whether to actualize our Christ potential [the Jesus of us] or allow it to remain unexpressed and dormant [He hid himself]. The choice, as always, is ours.

Pre-Christed Snapshot

37. Despite the experiencing of higher spiritual insights and divinely inspired ideas [miraculous signs] from time-to-time, which demonstrate our Christ potential [the Jesus of us], we still may have thoughts surface which come from an unenlightened egoic perspective [non-believers].

38. We must not judge ourselves too harshly during this phase of our unfoldment, because there is that within us, our evolving spiritual understanding [our Isaiahic capacity], which is attuned to our Christ Nature [Lord]. The Divine Presence [message] within us permeates our entire being [the arm of the Lord] and abides in us despite our unbelief.

39. Be assured that the Christ Presence is within us, even though we might not sense it. It is simply vibrating at a higher octave than our unenlightened egocentric awareness [they could not believe]. 40. Unless we raise our awareness to a Christed level of awareness, we will not comprehend [our eyes are blinded] nor be able to sense [our hearts are deadened] our true nature. As long as we deny our divinity [fail to see or understand], we will not unfold into our wholeness [be healed].

41. We know this about ourselves, because once we have heightened our awareness to a Christed level [our Isaiah capacity] we can see clear evi-

dence of our actualized Christ potential [Jesus' glory]. ⁴². We notice a change in our major belief systems [leaders]. However, we may still be prone to hold on to a number of ingrained beliefs and dogmas [our pharisaical perspective] which defined our old, ego-attached self. ⁴³. This is only natural since our pre-Christed awareness is filled with attachments to material things [our love and praise for men] instead of divinely-inspired thoughts, intentions, and choices [praise/glory from God].

The Omnipresent Ground of Being

⁴⁴. When our spiritually-evolved belief system [man] is based on the conviction that we have tremendous Christ potential [our Jesus quality], it follows that our thinking, being, and doing come from our Christ Nature [the one who sent me]. ⁴⁵ In a very true sense we are the face of God. ⁴⁶. The Cosmic Christ [the Light] is enfleshed in our consciousness [world], so we have an opportunity to move beyond the illusion [darkness] of our separation from Spirit.

⁴⁷. At the level of Spirit there is no consciousness of separation [no need for judgment], because at that Christed level of awareness there is only oneness and wholeness. There is no need to discern Truth from error [judge], because there is no error in spirit-filled consciousness [the world]. ⁴⁸. However, if we are the product of a sense-attached consciousness (one which denies our divinity), there is very definitely a need to discern Truth from error [judge]. Denying our divinity keeps us stuck in sense sludge [condemns us], which prevents us from moving to a higher level of awareness [the last day], and the broader perspective that comes with it. ⁴⁹. We know this at a deeper intuitive level [not of our own accord] because the Eternal Isness [the Father, (the One Reality, the Absolute)] is the omnipresent ground of our being. ⁵⁰. Make

no mistake about it, when we align our human personality with our Christ individuality, we shall attain Christ Consciousness [eternal life], and our life will demonstrate that divine *indivisibility*.

Chapter Thirteen

When Our Consciousness is Bathed in Spiritual Understanding

1. It is a truth well-known by those who have experienced it that going from one *cusp of consciousness* to another [a Passover experience], particularly from our ego or personality level of awareness [this world] to our higher, more Christed level of awareness [going to the Father], involves an extraordinary awakening. It means nothing less than completely harmonizing [loving] our entire thought universe [his own in the world] so that it resonates in every way with our innate perfection [the full extent of divine love/loved them to the end].

2. Spiritually unreceptive thoughts, beliefs, and biases [evening meal] are the fruits of a vehemently materialistic and unenlightened ego [devil], which prides itself in sense appetites [our Judas Iscariot propensity] that feed personal ambitions, not spiritual aspirations [our Simon leaning]. 3. Although personal ambition is the opium of a worldly ego, our Christ potential [the Jesus of us] gives us ready access to the allness of the Eternal Isness [Father, (the One Reality, the Infinite Invisibleness)]. Because we are the Eternal Isness [God] expressing at the point of us, we have the wherewithal to raise our awareness to a higher spiritual azimuth and become consciously one with the Eternal Isness [God (the One Reality, Absolute Good, the Eternal I-Am)]. 4. Our innate Christ potential [the Jesus of us] allows us to operate far above a consciousness of separation and lack [meal], by seeing through

the illusion of outer appearances [take off outer garments/clothing]. We can best attain this inner clarity by applying the life affirming knowledge of eternal truths [wrapping/tying a towel around waist]. 5. When we become one with the Indwelling Spiritual Life and Its effervescent energies [poured water], our consciousness [basin] and its unfolding spiritual energies [disciples] is filled with a high degree of spiritual understanding [washing feet]. The thoroughness of our understanding [drying the feet] will come from diligence and discipline as we apply higher knowledge [towel].

6. Our reluctance to move onward into new and higher orbits of spiritual awareness becomes obvious when we question the universality of substance, show our lack of faith [our undeveloped Simon Peter quality], and express disinterest in attaining more spiritual understanding [washing of feet].

7. We will need to be patient with ourselves as we move from an egocentric perspective to enlightened adeptship. 8. If our truth walk is not underwritten by faith [the Peter of us], our Christ potential [our Jesusness] will not unfold [be washed]. 9. Once we surrender to our Christ Nature and demonstrate our trust and faith [Simon Peter] in the transformative powers of our Christ potential, a deeper understanding [feet] and ability to craft [hands] a Christed outlook will go a long way toward the necessary reformation of our ego personality [head].

10. When we are resolved to walk the spiritual path [have been bathed], we need only increase our understanding [washed feet] of truth principles to elevate our consciousness [the whole body is clean]. However, until we are fully Christed, there will be aspects of our character that continue to be attached to sense appetites. 11. There is a part of us, our desire for sense attachments, which is prone to betray our quest for spiritual growth. Our 'skin school' attachments will con-

tinue to block our good until they are spiritually transformed.

12. When we have spiritually distilled our understanding so that it is a permanent part of our consciousness [finished washing feet], we can step out into the material world [put on clothes/robe] and remain *in* the world but not *of* the world. 13. By applying a consistently mature spiritual perspective [Teacher], we will consciously connect with our Christ Nature [Lord] and know that we are the Christ expressing *as* us. 14. Since our Christ potential is rooted in a powerfully rich spiritual mindset [Teacher] and has the Cosmic Christ [Lord] as its benefactor, we can use our new-found understanding [washed feet] to erase error-coated thoughts and beliefs lodged in our consciousness. 15. Our purpose in this incarnation, in any incarnation, is to be the best Christ [Example] we can be. 16. Worldly thoughts [servants/messengers] are always subordinate to spiritual insights [master/the one who sends]. 17. When our consciousness is consistently filled with spiritual thoughts and inclinations, we shall prosper [be blessed].

Truncating Our Spiritual Growth

18. It is not difficult to recognize a spirit-filled consciousness. However, until we have fully actualized our divinity [shared the bread], there will be times when we fail to comprehend the nuances of error [lift our heel] which truncate our spiritual growth.

19. We must understand our egocentric vulnerabilities so we can remind ourselves that we are spiritual beings on our way 'back home.' 20. When our body, mind, and soul work in concert with the truth of who we really are, we strengthen our connection with our Christ Nature.

21. If we are inconsistent in aligning our ego personality with our Christ individuality, we may compromise our Christ

potential [Jesus was troubled] by giving in to [betraying] sense attachments, particularly those which are covetous and overly consumptive.

22. Our spiritual energies and abilities [disciples], no matter how well developed, must be nurtured and honed if we are to reach adeptship. 23. If we expect to demonstrate our adeptship, we must maintain spiritual equilibrium and inner harmony [(John) the beloved disciple]. 24. Even our faith [Simon Peter] in Universal Supply may falter if our attention is focused on material gain. 25. We may even question our ability to achieve inner harmony and balance, despite knowing [leaning against Jesus] that we are beings with tremendous Christ potential.

26. Because we have so much Christ potential [the Jesus of us], the expanding awareness [piece of bread] of divine laws is readily available to us. Its absorption and receptivity [being dipped in the dish] depend on how attached we are to material appetites [our Judas Iscariot, son of Simon-ness]. 27. Unless we have highly developed qualities of discernment and spiritual intuition, there is that within us which denies our divinity [our satanic bent] and clings to such a belief in lack that it covets materiality [our aggrandizing Judasness] over spiritual growth. Although it can be one of the essential qualities of our spiritual growth when it is quickened, our Judas energy can become divisive if it fails to outgrow its consumptive fixation with material things.

28. The good news is that once our spiritual qualities are quickened and strengthened, we outgrow our need for chronic consumption and unnecessary acquisition. 29. If we allow ourselves to be driven by our sense consciousness [the Judas of us], we usually have a different view regarding the necessities of life [money/purse]. Our actions may appear to be consistent with our professed beliefs, but the motives are usually self-aggran-

dizing. ³⁰ What generally happens is that we give perfunctory attention to expanding our knowledge of divine laws [take the bread], and remain in the dark [night] when it comes to recognizing our true nature.

Our Newly Acquired Monistic Awareness

³¹· When we outgrow the centripetal force of sense consciousness [Judas is gone], we will reach a level of spiritual growth where we confidently and faithfully are able to determine the difference between Truth and error. This is possible because once we realize our Christ potential [glorify the Son of Man], our *Christship in potentiality* becomes manifested and *indivisiblized* God potency [God is glorified]. ³²· Once we achieve this level of adeptship [God is glorified in us], we literally become consciously one with the Cosmic Christ [the Son which God glorifies in himself]. This transmutation is instantaneous [glorified at once].

³³· Thoughts, attitudes, beliefs, and inclinations [children] which characterize our sense consciousness (coma consciousness) will no longer be part of our newly acquired Christed awareness.

³⁴· We must become good stewards of this newly acquired monistic awareness. At this heightened level of spiritual comprehension [new commandment], we must focus on and ensure that the inner harmonics which integrate [love] our expanded thought universe includes those 'ready-to-be-quickened' thoughts and beliefs which are the residue of our old thought climate. ³⁵· Once we undertake this purposeful integration, all of our quickening thoughts and beliefs [men] will unfold into their higher spiritual essences [disciples] and complete this phase of our harmonic convergence with our innate Christness.

36. Attaining this level of monistic awareness is a significant step on our spiritual journey. If our faith in the omnipresence of Divine Substance [our Simon Peter quality] is insufficiently quickened, and we have not intuited that consciousness is the ground of all being, we will be unable to comprehend the deeper insights associated with cosmic consciousness. Once we quicken that higher order quality, we will be able to grasp the sacred geometry of Spirit.

37. There is a difference between the faith [the Peter of us] that knows, and the desire to know, which is *wishcraft*. Each new level of cosmic awareness is faith-conditioned, which is to say the quality and maturity of our faith determine our readiness to move from one *cusp of consciousness* [lay down our life] to another.

38. Until we have matured in our faith, it will be difficult to shed old conditioning [lay down our life] for new spiritual depth and monist insights. If we remain caught up in the illusion of duality and separation, we will compromise the harmonious spiritualization of our body, mind, and soul [three denials]. This is the predictable outcome when we fail to follow our inner guidance [rooster/cock crows], which prompts us to "keep the faith!"

Chapter Fourteen

The Way, the Truth, and the Life

1. We do not have to vacillate between Truth and error, be uncertain about our inner wisdom, or fall out of harmony with our spiritual core [all aspects of a 'troubled heart']. We need only affirm that we are God expressing through the Christ *as* us.

2. Although the following languaging is insufficient in itself to convey the transcendentalness of God's presence, it will

serve to shed partial light on the omnipresence, omnipotence, omniscience, and onmiactivity of the One Reality (Eternal Isness, God, Divine Mind). In the totality of the Eternal Isness' quantum and cosmic beingness [Father's house], there are many levels of awareness or states of being [rooms/mansions]. It is through our actualized Christ potential (demonstrated by Jesus of Nazareth) that we are able to become one with that Truth [a place prepared for us].
3. Once we reach that level of Christed awareness (place of adeptship), as did Jesus of Nazareth, we will be able to align our waking conscious and subconscious with our spiritually-attuned super-conscious [take you to myself]. 4. By our very nature we are spiritual beings having human experiences. We are Christ embodied *as* us [we know the way (the incarnational path or expression)].

5. We cannot intellectualize this truth [depend solely on our Thomas energies] because the intellect requires physical proof and material confirmation. An unillumined intellect is the product of an unenlightened ego.

6. When we fully attain our Christhood, as did Jesus, we will obtain conscious *indivisibility* with the Cosmic Christ [the Way], God [the Truth] and the Holy Spirit [the Life]. It is through our conscious connection with the embodied Cosmic Christ (the Only Begotten Son) that we are able to attain conscious oneness with the One Reality [the Father].

7. Once we realize we are the Cosmic Christ expressing Itself *as* us, we will also discover that we are God (the One Reality, the Absolute) expressing Itself through the ensouled Cosmic Christ which underwrites all physicality.

8. Because we are spiritual beings housed in *quantum clothing* (physical bodies), we are prone to see duality and separation between us and our God Nature. It is from this limited vibrational awareness [our Phillip nature]

that we seek the Ultimate Truth [Father] behind the manifest and unmanifest universe.

9. What we must come to realize is that we *are* the universe becoming more conscious of itself. We must realize that it is consciousness that creates matter. We must realize that our ability to use the vibratory energies of the Universe [the Phillip of us] to create *something from nothing* (transform the formless into the formed) is possible because we are Spirit transfusing matter[a] 10. The same Christ that expressed Itself as Jesus expresses Itself *as* us. We are one with the Eternal Isness and the Eternal Isness [Father] expresses Itself *as* us. It is the One Reality (the Eternal Isness, the Infinite Invisibleness of Spirit) which underwrites our beingness in all phases (states of awareness) of our remembering who we are.

11. It cannot be overstated: We are the One Reality, the Eternal Isness [Father] expressing through the Cosmic Christ at the point of us. It is not at all difficult to sense that divine connection once we have experienced a given number of incarnations[b] in which we have gained extraordinary spiritual insights [miracles].

12. When we are faith-conditioned, and add to that the spiritual capital of a disciplined and reverential Truth walk, we will achieve an extraordinarily high level of awareness which will make it possible for us to exceed anything we could ever have accomplished at the level of the ego personality. Imagine what we could accomplish as a global society of Christs!

13. Whatever we declare [ask] from a Christed consciousness [in my name, (in the nature of)] will become manifested prosperity, because the formative power of the Cosmic Christ [Son] is always in alignment [glorifies] with Absolute Good [Father, (the One Reality, the Infinite Invisibleness)]. 14. When we reach that level

---
[a] *Quantumly speaking, this is 'collapsing the wave,' moving from wave (the unmanifest) to particle (the manifest).*
[b] *Incarnations, in and of themselves, are not necessary for re-establishing our divine origins. Incarnations are one of many paths of initiation.*

of adeptship, anything we affirm [ask] from our Christ Nature [in my name] becomes a demonstration of our oneness with Spirit (God expressing *as* us).

The Powerful Omniactivity of the Holy Spirit

15. Once we become one with the sacred harmony [love] that permeates the entire universe, our whole being resonates with that perfection (we will keep the commandments). 16. At the moment we become Christed (fully actualize our Christ potential as did Jesus of Nazareth), we open a latent cosmic filter (portal) that releases a powerful inner fire which has been called by many names – Comforter, Advocate, *paraclete, kundalini, ki, chi, N/um,* and Fire Spirit. 17. All of these refer to the sacred vehicle or Presence of Divine Omniactivity [Holy Spirit] expressing Itself *as* matter. Our ordinary human consciousness, which springs from the ego personality [world], cannot comprehend its Quantum Self[c] (higher, more enlightened self). The human personality finds it difficult to experience the movement of Spirit within.

18. Our human self (ego personality) is never orphaned by the Christ Presence within us. Instead, it is vivified and raised to its quantum essence (its higher spiritual vibration) by the vital energies of the Holy Spirit [I will come to you]. 19. Eventually, as we completely unfold into our Christhood, our ego personality will be integrated into its higher Quantum Self [the world will not see me anymore]. We will recognize that we are an embodied Christ, fully aware that we are Christ embodied.

20. At that juncture of our unfoldment [on that day], we realize we are God [Father] expressing through the Christ at the point of us, which makes us indivisible incarnations of the Christ embodied as us. 21. Our

---

[c] Our Quantum Self is the composite of all we have ever been in every dimension of our being, both manifest and unmanifest – pre-incarnational, incarnational, and post-incarnational. It is the Self which remembers our past lives and intra-dimensional lives.

True Self [whoever obeys my commandments] is the quantum expression of the Christ Self [the one who loves me]. And our Christ Self is the perfect Expression of God [Father (the Infinite Invisibleness)]. We will see that we are powered by the vital energies of the Holy Spirit (Comforter, Advocate, *paraclete, kundalini, ki, chi, n/um,* Fire Spirit).

22. We may ask ourselves, as a result of deep introspection [our Judas (not Judas Iscariot) quality], why our ego personality [the world] cannot comprehend higher truths.

23. It will eventually become evident that when we actualize our Christ potential [our Jesusness], we become consciously one with the One Reality [God] and live, move, and have our being from that Christed perspective. 24. On the other hand, it is the nature of our ego personality [the one who does not love me] to stay fixated in sense consciousness (coma consciousness), and thus, remain unaware of its relationship to its spiritual heritage. Our sense of this transpersonal dichotomy comes from our inner guidance [the Father who sent me].

25. This highly-charged, stereophonic spirituality has always been with us in potential [spoken while I am with you]. We sense Its vibration and feel Its presence throughout our unfoldment. 26. But when we achieve a Christed awareness, we will be able to harness the incredible power of the vital energies which emanate from the inner fire [Holy Spirit, Counselor, Advocate] within us.

27. When we become consciously one with the Christ Presence, we will experience complete and absolute alignment [peace] with our Christ Nature. It is a harmonization and synchronicity with cosmic bliss that we will never experience through the ego personality. There will be no need to vacillate [be troubled] between Truth and error, because error will be non-existent in our elevated state of awareness.

28 When we raise our consciousness to the Christ Standard, elevating it above egocentric awareness [I am going away], we make it possible for those elevated energies to permeate [come back] our entire consciousness. We have this assurance because we are divine expressions of God [the Father (the One Reality, the Eternal Isness)] at the point of us. 29. Since we are aware of our Higher Self and Its transformative powers, we can prepare ourselves to be the best Christs we can be.

30. As we move closer to the moment of our fully ordained Christship, the ego personality [the prince of this world] will resist its absorption into our Christ individuality. However, our Christ Nature shall prevail. 31. Our ego personality [the world] will metamorphasize into its true spiritual nature and, once it is aligned with the embodied Christ, become fertile spiritual soil for the divine harmonics [love] which is set into motion by the Holy Spirit. We become consciously reunited with the Eternal Isness [Father, (the One Reality, the Infinite Invisibleness, Spirit)], recognizing that, in truth, we have never been separated [have done exactly what was commanded].

Chapter Fifteen

Our Christ Self, the True Vine

1. The Christ [I Am, (the Only Begotten Son)] embodied as us is our True Self [the True Vine], and the Eternal Isness [Father] is the Ground of All Being [the Husbandman, Vine-Grower, Gardener]. 2 Every spiritual potentiality [branch] that atrophies [is cut off] does not bear divine ideas [fruit]. However, when we actualize our spiritual potential [branch], we receive divine ideas [fruit] which can be used [pruned] to generate more divine ideas [be more fruitful].

3. We have constant access to divine ideas [we are already clean/cleansed] because we are the Indwelling Christ [Word] expressing Itself *as* us [I have spoken to you]. 4. When we actualize our Christ potential [remain, abide in me], we align ourselves with our God Nature [I remain, abide in you]. All of our divine potential [branches], and the spiritual ideas [fruit] it generates, comes from the Christ Presence within us. If we fail to unfold into our Christ potential, we will delay our Christological inheritance.

5. It is important to remind ourselves that the Christ [the Eternal I Am] is our True Self [the Vine], and that It is the Source of our spiritual potential [branches]. If we align our human thoughts with our Christ Self, we will intuit many spiritual ideas and insights [bear much fruit]. 6. If we settle for a consciousness which is not Christed, we are prone to neglect our spiritual potential [a branch thrown away]. When we make such a mis-step, our spiritual potential remains latent within us as an untapped, purifying force [a branch thrown into the fire].

7. Once we live, move, and have our being from a Christed perspective [remain in me], whatever we affirm from that elevated state of awareness will become part of our human experience. 8. It is this oneness with our I Am Nature [the Father's glory] that brings us many divine revelations [fruit], which can only come from a consciousness that has highly developed spiritual qualities [disciples].

9. As the Eternal Isness [Father, (the One Reality, Divine Mind)] is one with the Cosmic Christ [loves me], so the Christ is one with us. Knowing this, we must do all we can to align our thinking with that truth. 10. When we consciously seek to stay in sync with our Christness by consistently applying divine principles [obey the commandments], we will stay in harmony

[remain / abide, in my love] with our Christ Nature, which is the Eternal Self [Father] embodied as us.

11. It is important to realize that the *wholing* and harmonizing qualities [joy] of the Indwelling Spirit (the Cosmic Christ) are readily available to us. 12 Our disciplined adherence to divine principles [commandments] makes it possible for us to harmonize [love] our human self and Christ Self [each other/ one another]. 13. No greater symetrization [love] is possible than to transform [lay down] the best of our human qualities [one's life] for the higher qualities [friends] of Spirit.

14. The demonstration of these higher qualities [friends] is possible once we align ourselves with divine principles [commandments]. 15. When we reach this level of adeptship, we tend to outgrow sense attachments [servants] because sense attachments [servants] are not the products of a disciplined truth practitioner's journey [the master's business, what the Lord doeth]. Instead, we strive to cultivate higher spiritual qualities [friends], which characterize our conscious oneness with the One Reality [the Father, (the Absolute)].

16. Our lower, more worldly thoughts are not in sync [did not choose] with higher spiritual principles; however, when we tighten our synchronization [choose you, make known to you] with Spirit, we will receive divine ideas [fruit] that can transform our belief system [fruit that lasts]. As has been said before, when we declare our good in the name of the living Christ by affirming our oneness with the Eternal Isness [the Father, (the Infinite Invisibleness)], we will be able to form out of the formless unlimited prosperity and wealth. 17. This is based on a Universal Truth [commandment]: Harmonize [love] our human self with our Christ Self [each other] so that their *indivisibleness* is recognized and demonstrated. (Another way of

It Doesn't Make Sense to Deny Our Innate Divinity

[18] Sense consciousness [the world] is so rooted in matter that it is oblivious to [hates] any connection we have with Spirit. [19.] If all we are is flesh and blood [belong to the world], we would only resonate with the material appetites of a self-absorbed ego and sense-addicted consciousness [the world]. But the truth is, we are spiritual beings having a human experience. And it is our unenlightened resistance to our innate divinity which causes us to deny [hate] any spiritual thought, inclination, or insight which threatens our egocentricity.

[20.] We must remember this important truth: a material thought [servant] will always be less powerful than a spiritual insight [master]. If we allow worldly thoughts to deter us [persecute us] from right thinking, we defer our spiritual growth. On the other hand, once our thoughts and inclinations are Christ-centric [we obey teachings], the effect on our overall consciousness is positive and life-affirming. [21.] Egocentric thoughts characterize our resistance to our divine nature [they do not know the One who sent me]. Such a worldly frame of reference limits the awareness of our real nature [name], which is divine.

[22.] When our thoughts and inclinations are Christ-centric, they are in perfect alignment with spiritual laws [they are sinless]. Whether our thoughts and inclinations continue to exemplify our spiritual commitment [are not guilty of sin (misalignment)] depends on us.

[23.] When we deny [hate] the Christ *as* us, we deny [hate] our oneness with the One Reality [Father, (the Eternal Isness, the Infinite Invisibleness)] as well. [24.] If we continue to use the richness and vitality of our spiritual attributes and powers, which are far superior to the qualities of our ego personality, we will stay in sync with the vital energies of spiritual laws [not be guilty of sin (misalignment)]. If we choose to neglect the transformative effects of higher consciousness' distinctive *signatures* [miracles] after experiencing them, for all intents and purposes, we deny [hate] our divine heirship (*indivisibleness* with the [Father]). [25.] This abject denial [written in their (worldly) law (awareness)] seems to be a characteristic of sense consciousness.

[26.] Be assured, however, that deep within us lie the *kundalini* energies [the Advocate, Counselor (Fire Spirit, *ki, chi,* Holy Spirit)]. These latent energies are the omniactive vital energies of the One Reality [Father]. They lie at the base of our spine waiting to rise [testify] through the power centers of our spine to our head. When we experience this ascent [testimony], we will become a walking, living, breathing Christ, fully conscious of our Christness as did Jesus the Nazarene.

Chapter Sixteen

Our Sense-Corrupted Thoughts and Beliefs Must Go

[1.] It may seem unnecessary to make the following statement, but it must be made: Spiritual principles must be applied if we are to grow spiritually. [2.] Ironically, when we apply higher truths they invariably come into conflict with encrusted religious biases [synagogue]. Indeed, during the initial stages of our unfoldment [a time is coming], we may deny [kill] the expression of a particular spiritual quality and believe we are in sync [offering a service, worshipping] with our I-Am-ness [God] by using materialistic means to achieve spiritual ends. [3.] Such actions are sense-corrupted actions [they do not know the Father (God)]. [4.] We must be aware of the influence of our past programming and its egocentric origins. When we are in a high state of consciousness, our egocentrism does not come into play. Our challenge, in our normal waking awareness, is to remember who we really are.

The Holy Spirit's Sushumnic Effect

5. At the moment our Christ potential is actualized [I am going to him who sent me], we generally do not comprehend the immense change which has taken place [none asks "Where are you going?"] 6. Although we have anticipated this moment, we are prone to pine over [are filled with grief] a few hard-to-release sense attachments. 7. It is important to know at this juncture of our unfoldment that our Christ potential must give way [I must go away] to a fuller demonstration of our Christhood. If that does not happen, we will not develop the skills and awarenesses we need to call forth the serpentine energies [the Advocate, Counselor, (Fire Spirit, *kundalini*, Holy Spirit)] which lie latent within us, waiting for expression. 8. When we experience the rise of the Inner Fire (Holy Spirit), Its *sushumnic* potency signifies our liberation from the illusion of separation and duality which has been fabricated by our sense consciousness [the world of guilt] to perpetuate the ego's rulership. There are three things we should know about the nature of this liberation and they involve a conversation about error thinking [sin], the right use of spiritual laws [righteousness], and surrendering to the guidance of the 'still small voice' [judgment]. 9. We are subject to error thinking [sin] if we neglect or deny our innate divinity [do not believe]. 10. Once we raise our awareness to the Christ Standard [go to the Father], the right use of spiritual laws [righteousness] depends on our ability to keep our ego personality in check [see me no longer]. 11. Keeping our ego [the prince of this world] in check by paying close attention to the inner promptings of the 'still

small voice' [judgment] will be the most difficult transition to make, because the ego does not want to relinquish [stand condemned] its temporal rulership.

12. We have much to learn about the nature of our liberation, and we can be sure the clarity will come when we are truly ready to claim our Christogenic heirship. 13. And when we reach that point in our awareness, the Holy Spirit's *sushumnic* potency will vitalize our entire being [tell us what is to come] with Its sacred inner fire. 14. These highly-charged serpentine energies will fuel our enlightenment [bring glory] by ramping up our awareness to the highest spiritual orbit we have ever experienced. 15. When we reach that pinnacle of Christed awareness, we will see and feel the quantum muscle of the Absolute [the Father (God, Eternal Isness, the Infinite Invisibleness)]. In this extraordinarily high orbit of receptivity, we will experience the allness of the One Reality (Absolute, [God]) because God desires gods.

16. We will have turned Christ potential [you will see me no more] into Christ perfection [you will see me again].

Less Lag Time, More Real Time

17. Our spiritual qualities [disciples] will remain at a plateau if we do not turn their potential good [see me no more] into quickened development [see me again]. Quickening our spiritual qualities requires withdrawing from the world [going to the Father] through meditation, prayer, and disciplined study. 18. Each time we elevate our awareness to a Christed awareness, we leave the world of sense and enter the realm of super-conscious awareness. It is the lag time [a little while] between ego awareness and Christed awareness that we must eliminate in order to keep our energies at a super-conscious level.

19. Because we have incredible Christ potential [the Jesus of us], our vital energies pull us toward establishing permanent

residence in our super-conscious awareness without any leakage into our egocentric awareness.
20. Each time we slip out of our Christed orbit, we relegate ourselves to the limitations imposed by our egocentric awareness. We 'weep and mourn' (lose our connection) while the world (sense consciousness) rejoices (dominates our awareness)]. When we are in sync through meditation and prayer, we transform ego awareness [grief] into Christed awareness [joy].

21. Our attempts to live at the speed of our Christ Consciousness are like the intuitive process [woman] of ideating [giving birth] a divine idea [child]. The process itself can be laborious [painful]. It is the nature of the process [her time has come]. But when the idea arrives [the child/baby is born], we forget the toilsome process because the joy of the "aha" experience [a child is born] makes it all worth while.

22. So, we must remind ourselves that when we find ourselves out of sync [a time of grief] with our Higher Self, all we need to do is get back into alignment to experience the joy of the Christ Connection.

23. Every time [in that day] we raise our awareness to the Christ Standard, whatever we affirm [ask] from that elevated awareness [Father, (the One Reality)] shall be so. 24. We reach that elevated state of awareness when we affirm our oneness [ask in my name] with Spirit and remain constantly aware of that connection. Affirmations from a Christed awareness generate incredible vibrational power to fuel our ability to manifest our greater good.

No More Need For Involution or Evolution

25. When we reach a Christed level of awareness [the hour/time is coming], we will have moved beyond any struggle to discern Truth from error [use figurative language, dark sayings] because we will have at-

tained Christ Consciousness. 26. Because our awareness is raised to a more quantum awareness [on that day], our affirmations and declarations [asking] will all come from an illumined consciousness, which has turned Christ potential into God [Father] expressing without the encumbrance of ego filters.

27. We are consciously one with [loved by] the One Reality [Father himself]. We have completely harmonized [loved] our human self with our Divine Self. We have no doubt that God [Father, (the Absolute)] expresses Itself through the Cosmic Christ *as* us.

28. This is the great truth associated with the human experience: The Cosmic Christ, as the formative aspect of the One Reality [Father], became enfleshed in human consciousness [the world] and in all matter. As we come into this realization, our overall awareness of the innate divinity of humankind is raised [I leave the world] to the degree that we individually become illumined. As each one of us becomes enlightened, there will come a time when the Cosmic Christ no longer has to underwrite the material universe because matter and Spirit will vibrate once again [go back] in sync with the Eternal Isness [Father]. There will be no need for physicality, no need for involution or evolution, because the concepts of error, evil, separation, and duality will not exist. All will be pure Spirit once again.[a]

29. Upon full illumination [now you are speaking clearly], all of our spiritual abilities [disciples] will have become quickened [are without figures of speech/without dark sayings]. 30. We will have reached that place of absolute certainty that we are God [Father, (the Eternal Isness)] expressing Itself through the Christ *as* us.

31. Once we fully realize our Christhood [believe at last], we become consciously whole and complete. 32. Our ego personality, with its hordes of error

---

[a] *Quantumly speaking, there will be no collapse of the 'wave.'*

thoughts, will be dissolved [we will be scattered] and our Christ Individuality will dominate our illumined consciousness [each has gone home]. Christ-centric thinking will define our elevated consciousness.

33. At this level of illumination we will have mastered our egocentric human experience [overcome the world].

Chapter Seventeen

We Must See Jesus as the Perfect Example, Not the Great Exception

1. There will come a time when our Christ potential [the Jesus of us] will become fully actualized [he looked toward heaven], and our communion [prayer] with the Indwelling Presence will have aligned our human personality with our Christ Individuality [glorified the Son (the Christ)]. It will be clear to us that we are the Christ [Son] expressing at the point of us, and that the Christ is God [the Father, (the One Reality)] expressing Itself as the Perfect Idea (the Cosmic Christ) in the quantum universe (physicality).

2. We will have no doubt that the Christ, as Cosmic Principle, underwrites all physicality [has universal authority] and that Christ Consciousness [eternal life] is available to all who seek the enlightened path. 3. Our ability to achieve Christ Consciousness [eternal life] has already been demonstrated by the Christ as Jesus [Jesus Christ] the man from Nazareth, born of Joseph and Mary, who fully actualized his Christhood and became fully conscious of his oneness with the One Reality [the only true God].

4. Through his thoughts, words, and actions, Jesus became consciously one with his Christ Self [brought glory on earth] by transforming his ego personality into his Christ Individuality.

5. We can demonstrate Christhood by following Jesus' example. We can affirm with absolute conviction that the same Cosmic Christ that expressed Itself *as* Jesus is the same Cosmic Christ that is the formative aspect of the One Reality [the Father]. This Cosmic Isness is the Infinite Invisibleness out of which spiritual beings have, and are, creating the physical universe. We *are* that same eternal, timeless Cosmic Christ expressing Itself *as* us, as well as our children, grandchildren, and great grandchildren, and their offspring. That is the message of Jesus, and that is the message of the manuscript you are holding.

Enfiring Our Thoughts, Words, and Actions

6. Because we have awesome Christ potential, we are endowed with certain spiritual qualities [disciples] which vibrate at a high resonance [obey your word] through the somatic filters of our waking consciousness. 7. When we see the world through our higher spiritual qualities, as did Jesus, we know that everything we are able to be, do, and have comes from Spirit (the One Reality, God, the Infinite Invisibleness). 8. As we conscientiously unfold our Christ potential by applying the truth principles we know, we gain the higher knowledge which comes from our Christ Connection. 9. When we access these higher spiritual qualities, we accelerate our ability to harmonize [pray] our energies with our Christ potential. 10. We must trust that our spiritually-charged qualities, insights, and ideas come to us because we come pre-wired with Christ potential. These latent potentialities are what make our unfoldment [glory] possible.

11. Once we actualize our Christ potential [no longer remain in the world (sense consciousness)], our Christed qualities, insights, and ideas will continue to permeate our entire consciousness [remain in the

world]. Our Christ-in-potential status becomes Christ in-actuality [we go to the Holy Father (the One Reality, God)]. And so, by the very nature [name] of our Christed awareness, we are able to master [are protected] the human experience. We become consciously one with our Christ Self [the name given to us], which is our True Self.

12. Even before we fully actualize our Christ potential [while I was still with them], we receive promptings from our Christ Self [the name given to us]. We are fortified [protected] by our higher spiritual qualities (disciples) as we walk a disciplined spiritual path; however, we are still prone to the sense attachments of our covetous acquisitive nature [the one (Judas) doomed to destruction/to be lost]. Our journey from covetousness to a fully awakened consciousness [the *scripture* (of our evolving awareness)] is one which must play itself out [be fulfilled] as we fully embody our divinity.

13. As our Christ potential becomes fully actualized [I am coming to you now], it signifies our quickening powers of discerning Truth from error. Although we are still matriculating through sense attachments [I am still in the world], we are on our way toward developing a fully Christed awareness [a full measure of joy].

14. We must understand the hydraulic relationship between sense appetites and spiritual growth: the more we are the products of sense appetites, the less we will strive to be the best Christ [word] we can be. A sense-driven, egocentric personality [the world] tends to deny [hate] our innate divinity. Therefore, neither our Christed thoughts nor our Christ potential are honored [not of the world] in a sense-soaked consciousness.

15. An important point must be made in consideration of the previous text. By no means are we to see separation between our human self and our Christ Self

[take them out of the world]. Our evolutionary task is to tame an unenlightened ego [the evil one]. [16.] Christed thoughts do not spring from a consciousness fixated on material appetites [the world] and error does not exist in a Christed consciousness. [17.] We must align [sanctify] ourselves with the perennial Christ Presence [Truth]. [18.] Because our Christ potential is infolded in our consciousness [the world], our higher spiritual qualities (disciples) are also present. [19.] When our Christ potential is in complete alignment [is sanctified] with our Christ Self, our higher spiritual qualities (disciples) will also be aligned [truly sanctified] with our Christ Self.

We Are Christed at Our Core

[20.] Quickening our higher spiritual thoughts, qualities, and abilities (disciples) leads to the quickening of other, more sense-prone, human qualities and traits. [21.] As we continue to unfold, all of our thoughts, qualities, and abilities will become Christed so that our entire consciousness [the world] will be in alignment with our God Nature [Father, (God, the One Reality)]. [22.] Since our thoughts and inner qualities are already Christed at their core [are glorified], we need only quicken them. [23.] When we acknowledge our innate divinity, we can harmonize [bring to complete unity] our thoughts, feelings, and abilities.

[24.] Our purpose, as spiritual beings in human form, is to become consciously one with our Christ Self [to see my glory] which is the Cosmic Christ. Our Christ potential was guaranteed before the material universe was formed, because we have been Christed beings from the beginning.[a]

[25.] Even though we may choose to remain a product of an egocentric consciousness [the world] which does not resonate with our divine heirship, we can

---

[a] *In the invisible, non-collapsed, quantum world of Spirit, we were spiritual beings before we became embodied in matter.*

be assured that we are Christed at our core. ²⁶ Enlightenment is in our spiritual DNA, and our innate divinity [the love you have for me] is our birthright.

Chapter Eighteen

The Acoustics of Betrayal

¹· As long as we remain in an elevated state of consciousness [pray], we honor our Christ potential [the Jesus of us] and fortify our spiritual qualities [disciples]. However, even at this level of heightened awareness we will have many opportunities to move past sense appetites [cross the Kidron Valley], as we struggle to eliminate any and all worldly attachments [a Gethsemane (olive grove) experience]. ²· No matter how illumined we may think we are, the struggle to erase the staining effects of error [betrayal by our aggrandizing Judasness] will occupy more of our time than we might think. ³· This fixation with material appetites [our Judas penchant] produces mercenary thoughts [soldiers and police] and dogmatic biases [chief priests and pharisaical states of mind], which are characterized by intellectual thirst for worldly knowledge [lanterns], caustic pragmatism [torches], and fear-laced self-preservation [weapons].

⁴· If we remain steadfast and honor the Christ *as* us [our Jesus Christ capacity] in the face of human dramas, we will understand the implications of compromising our integrity ["who do you want?"] and choose a more Christed path.

⁵· If we are out of alignment with our true nature, we may tend to identify with our human self (ask for Jesus of Nazareth). But we must stand firm in the knowledge of who we really are, recognizing that our human self [I am he] and our Christ Self are one, despite our struggle with our acquisitive nature [the Judas of us]. ⁶· Rest assured, the moment we know in our heart

of hearts that we are one with our True Self [the Christ], our human attachments will take a subordinate role [they withdrew and fell to the ground].

7. We must decide who we want to be, merely our human self or our Christ Self ["Who is it you want?"]. Identifying with our humanness only and neglecting to actualize our Christ potential [the Jesus of us] will keep us on incarnational and reincarnational merry-go-rounds.

8. If we see ourselves as mere human beings, we will miss opportunities to quicken our higher spiritual qualities [let these men go]. 9. However, we do not lose our spiritual attributes, even if they remain latent within us.

10. If we have not quickened our faith [the Simon Peter of us], we may tend to misuse knowledge of the Truth [sword]. For example, we may purposefully refuse to heed a spiritual intuition [cut off right ear] because we fail to see its merits, especially if we are prone to follow established convention [high priest's servant / slave]. Questioning the value of any potentially viable spiritual perspective [the Malchus of us], no matter how benign it may seem, generally dims our spiritual perspective.

11. If we remain true to our Christ potential [the Jesus of us] and deepen our faith [the Peter of us], we will use our knowledge of truth principles [the sword] wisely and prudently.

A Treacherous Sense-Entranced Ego

12. We must be under no illusion that the closer we are to fully expressing our Christ Nature, the more pronounced will be the ego's controlling tendencies [detachment of soldiers] and dogmatic rigidity [Jewish officials]. 13. This vicious resistance comes from a sense-entranced ego [the Annas of us], which will mount considerable intellectual opposition [the Caiaphas of us] to arrest any inkling of our divine connection. 14. When we take our divinity for granted, a subversive

intellect [our Caiaphas weakness] will seek to dampen [kill] any spiritual inclination [man] which hints at our divine origins.

We Must Prime Our Unprimed Faith

15. As we deepen our commitment to our truth walks, the two qualities which are essential to that unfoldment are an evolving faith [our Simon Peter quality] and a love for the Truth [the John of us]. It is our love for the Truth [the disciple (John)] that frustrates a worldly intellect [the high priest (Caiaphas)], which knows all too well how to stifle an inner impulse by treating it as merely a perfunctory urge. Our unquickened intellect operates with an air of built-in alienation [the high priest's courtyard] when it comes to comprehending anything it finds difficult to quantify in material terms. 16. The more pronounced our love for the Truth is [the other disciple], the more apt we are to tap into our unquickened, but blossoming, intuitive intelligence [the woman/girl]. Our unprimed faith [the immature Peter of us] generally keeps us too reticent [at the door] to be proactive in the face of difficult circumstances.

17. Unsure of ourselves, we may question the validity of our faith [the immature Peter of us]. 18. Even though our faith [our Peterness] may waiver [it is cold], we must find it within ourselves, despite any submissiveness [servants/slaves] or institutionalized rigidity [officials] we may feel, to connect with the Indwelling Presence (find warmth).

The Harshness of a Dogmatic Perspective

19. In spite of its dominance as a product of our ego personality, our unenlightened intellect [the high priest] cannot comprehend the growing influence of our Christ Nature [the Jesus of us] or the strength of our quickening spiritual abilities [disciples]. 20. What an unen-

lightened intellect fails to grasp is that the Truth has always been present in our consciousness [the world], despite being hidden in traditional interpretations of scripture [synagogues and temples] and benign religious teachings, or repressed by a chronically obsessed irreligious attitude in general. [21.] We do not need to question the legitimacy of our evolving spiritual portfolio.[a] The effect our quickened spiritual abilities have on our normal abilities and attributes will become increasingly obvious as we experience their Christed energies throughout our incarnational experiences.

[22.] The harshness of an encrusted dogmatic perspective [official] causes us to recoil from the clarity we can gain [striking the face] if we allow ourselves to openly and enthusiastically embrace the Truth which is staring us in the face.

[23.] It is important for us to be able to discern Truth from error. If we are truly seeking the Truth [if I spoke the Truth], why would we rail against the clarity it brings [strike the face]? [24.] The answer is fairly straightforward: We allow a recalcitrant ego [the Annas of us] to subvert [bind] the Truth by using a nihilistic intellect [our Caiaphas destructive nature] to hide it.

Denying Our Christ Connection

[25.] As has been mentioned previously, if we allow ourselves to be overly influenced by the world of outer appearances, we may tend to question the strength of our faith [our Simon Peterness]. [26.] It has been mentioned before that if we are prone to question the viability of any spiritual perspective (the Malchus of us), we may be unduly influenced by another equally error-ridden line of reasoning [a relative of Malchus] as we struggle to eliminate worldly attachments [an olive grove experience]. [27.] If we get to the point where we adamantly deny our connection with Spirit because we feel pressured by the slings and arrows

---
[a] *Our incarnational ('skin school') experiences.*

of outer appearances, we will experience an incredibly disconcerting inner alarm [rooster/cock crows] which signals our failure to walk our talk. If our faith degenerates to that point, we have essentially compromise meaningful spiritual growth.

Choosing to Align or Rebel Against Our Christ Nature

28. When we allow ourselves to follow self-righteous, judgmental instincts [enter the Praeorium], we repress our Christ potential [the Jesus of us] by giving in to a subversive intellect [our Caiaphasness] which is willful and regimented [the Roman governor (the Pilate of us)] in its unreceptivity to Spirit. This limited perspective [early morning] thrives on intellectual rigidity [our unillumined Jewishness] and demands absolute adherence to strict conventional protocols (avoids ceremonies, considered as defilements). As long as we remain attached to worldly appetites, we will not be able to understand [eat] higher, more esoteric teachings or go from an unillumined human awareness to a super-conscious awareness [a Passover experience] of who we really are. 29. Interestingly, from a purely self-aggrandizing point of view [our Pilate penchant], we may perfunctorily explore higher spiritual qualities simply for their perceived value in maximizing our worldly attachments. 30. Our interest is usually mercenary because we want to strengthen any quality which fortifies our own egocentric self-interests.

31. If we continue our self-centered trek through life [our Pilate perspective], we will see esoteric wisdom as an amusing sideline, something to be played with, but not taken seriously. In spite of this fractured perspective, we intuitively sense there may be innate value associated with higher qualities, value which is beyond the ego's sense-soaked grasp. 32. No matter how fond we are of material appetites, there is a deeply intuitive spiritual instinct within us which triggers an unexplainable inner

knowing. This interior refinement prompts us to consider that we are here to cross out error [be crucified] so we can rise above our human frailties.

33. However, as long as we continue to choose flesh over Spirit [enter the Praetorium] and mindlessly express our penchant for self-aggrandizement [the Pilate of us], we will remain uneasy with the notion that there is a ruling Spiritual Presence within us [the King of the Jews] which could usurp the ego's rulership of our human personality.

34. If we are consciously one with our Christ Nature [the Jesus of us], we know that the ego merely wants confirmation of its rulership over the lower, more temporal aspects of our human nature.

35. We also know that our self-aggrandizing, carnal will [our Pilateness] is, as yet, an unquickened spiritual quality [our unillumined Jewishness] which, although misguided, is following its urge to become perfect and whole.

36. Our spiritually-quickened thought universe [the Kingdom] vibrates at a much higher octave than our ego consciousness [the world]. If our ego consciousness were fully Christed, our thoughts [servants/followers] would be in alignment [prevent my arrest] with our Christ Nature and raise any and all unquickened spiritual thoughts [our unillumined Jewish bent] to their higher vibrations.

37. The interesting thing about an unenlightened ego is that when we affirm our oneness with our Christ Self [king], it cannot comprehend the implications of such an affirmation of faith. Until our ego comes into alignment with its higher, more Christed essence, we will not see that the Cosmic Christ became enfleshed *as* us in human form to raise our soul vibration to its spiritual essence [to testify to the Truth].

38. In our deluded self-centeredness [the Pilate of us], we question what at-one-ment with our Divine Nature [Truth] means, suspecting there may be

more to us than mere flesh and blood [I find no basis for a charge against him]. ³⁹·So, we have a decision to make. Do we seek to understand the Presence of God [the King of the Jews] within, so we can rise above error [a Passover experience]? ⁴⁰·Or do we hold onto our rebelliousness [our Barabbas nature] to appease a willful ego intent on protecting its sense-bound rulership by keeping our human personality unaware of its divine origins?

Chapter Nineteen

When Our Egocentric World View Twists the Truth

¹·If we allow our sense appetites to rule our personality, our willfulness in its most worldly form [the Pilate of us] will seek to discredit [flog] any notion of our having Christ potential [the Jesus of us]. ²·We may even go so far as to twist the Truth [weave a crown of thorns] to suit our mercenary aims [soldiers], since our intent is to protect our egocentric world view [place crown on head], which is the product of a fundamentally entrenched materialistic perspective [the scarlet/purple robe]. ³·If our lives are defined by egocentrism, we may even mock the possibility of our divine heirship [Hail, King of the Jews] by attacking the very notion of our innate Godness [striking him in the face].

⁴·In a most dauntless, yet condescending manner [the Pilate of us], we are prone to discount paying any serious attention to our spiritual development [I find no case against him] by patronizing our worldly bents [our unillumined Jewishness]. ⁵·Although we are beings with tremendous Christ potential [the Jesus of us], we conceal it under a veneer of an egocentric world view [crown of thorns] and materialistic cravings [purple robe].

⁶·As long as we remain the products of glaucomic spirituality [chief priests] and parochial religious biases [officials/police],

we are prone to ridicule any notion that there are errors we have to correct [crucify him]. Our disinterest stems from a materialistic willfulness [our Pilateness] which springs from a cul-de-saced worldly perspective.

7. At this level of truncated awareness [our worldly Jewish perspective], we generally operate under the assumption [law] that a spiritual perspective has no place [must die] in a material world. This view is reinforced by the false belief that we are not the Christ [Son of God] expressing *as* us.

8. Despite our worldliness [the Pilate of us], we have a sense that there is more to us than our humanness. 9. From a worldly perspective [palace], we cannot conceive of what it means to have Christ potential [the Jesus of us]. 10. As long as we are the products of a materialistic willfulness [our Pilateness], we will not see that a worldly consciousness limits us while a spiritually-quickened consciousness prospers us.

11. And yet, from a Christed perspective [our Jesus quality] we know that our materialistic bents [the Pilate of us] are simply lower vibrations of the Real us, which has been repressed by a paranoid ego [the one who handed me over] burdened [guilty] by the denial [the greater sin] of our innate divinity.

12. Until we fully actualize our Christ potential [free Jesus], we will be unduly influenced by worldly thoughts [our unillumined Jewish nature] which surface. These temporal thoughts indicate our desire to identify ourselves more with our earthy grandiose bents [the Caesar of us] than our divine heritorship.

13. It is from this immovable state of sensory addiction [a Gabbatha / Stone Pavement perspective] that we forget about [take Jesus outside] our divine connection. 14. Although the opportunity still exists for us to elevate our awareness to a more Christed perspective [preparation for Passover], we choose instead to see duality and separa-

tion [the sixth hour/noon]. By our very thoughts, words, and actions, we mock our divinity ["Here is our King."].

15. Unfortunately, if our consciousness is defined by its egocentric narcissism, we tend to pride ourselves in grandiose materialism [have no king but Caesar] and generally refuse to 'cross out' material addictions we view as harmless consumptions.

16. However, if we want to give up the limitations associated with our material nature [the Pilate of us], we must surrender [be crucified] to our Christ Nature.

Crossing Out Error in All Three Planes of Consciousness

17. When we allow our Christness to manifest in our humanness [carry our own cross], we essentially give up our egocentric personality and claim our Christ Individuality [go to Golgotha, the Place of the Skull]. This transformation takes place in our head (the Place of the Skull). It means raising our awareness to a Christed level of awareness. 18. Our belief in duality and separation [two robbers] is no longer part of our consciousness. 19. The distinction of the human personality [Jesus of Nazareth] and the Christ Personality [King of the Jews] gives way to a consciousness of oneness, since the previously inharmonious energies within us [our Pilate discontinuities] are adjusted to their right relationship [fastened to the cross] with Spirit (our I-Am-ness, our Christ Self). 20. When we are fully attuned to our higher spiritual dimension [the Jews read the sign/inscription], we will have unfolded into our Christ-likeness on all three levels of consciousness: the super-conscious [Aramaic/Hebrew], subconscious [Latin], and waking conscious [Greek]. 21. Even at this level of heightened awareness, dogmatic thoughts [chief priests] may surface. We may question the validity of our emerging Christ Personality [do not write

King of the Jews but claim to be King of the Jews]. 22. But these thoughts come from a worldly personality [the Pilate of us] which cannot grasp our Christness.

23. On the other hand, when we are in absolute and total sync with our Christ Nature, there is no consciousness of separation [seamless garment] between our Christed Self and our emotional, mental, physical, and spiritual selves [dividing clothes into four shares / parts].[a]

24. The One Life [the Cosmic Christ] becoming fully actualized in one of us (as demonstrated by Jesus of Nazareth) becomes part of the spiritual experience of the many [divided garments]. Each of us, as incarnated souls [the casting of the lots], has the opportunity to raise our consciousness to its Christed orbit.

25. As we deepen our spirituality, there are three inner qualities which can help solidify our ability to cross out error. They are: superior intuition [Mary, mother of Jesus], the ability to divinely order our experience [Mary, wife of Clopas], and our uncompromised devotion to loving service [Mary Magdalene]. 26. As we become more grounded in our Christed awareness [our Jesusness], we will find that the connection between superior intuition (Mary) and the harmonizing and healing energies of love [the beloved disciple] 27. must be one of impeccability, closeness, and constancy.

Mastering Our Incarnational 'Calling'

28. From a super-conscious *indivisibility* which is out-pictured as our divine nature [scripture being fulfilled], we *thirst* for complete at-one-ment with God (the One Reality, the Infinite Invisibleness). 29. The bitterness [sour wine, wine vinegar, (minty bitter) hyssop] of our self-imposed incarnational sojourn gives way to the sweetness of

---
[a] *Dividing clothes into shares/parts can also refer to the disbursement of the Christ energy and vitality to the four corners of the world: north, east, south, and west.*

our conscious oneness with Spirit. [30.] It becomes clear to us that we have mastered our incarnational 'calling'[b] ["It is finished"]. We have subordinated our ego personality [bowed his head] and raised our awareness to its quantum monism [gave up his spirit].

[31.] At this elevated Christed perspective [the day of Preparation], we have overcome [a Sabbath experience] our temporal, egocentric nature so there is no error to cross out of our consciousness [no bodies left on crosses]. However, until we come to that heightened awareness, our thoughts are still centered in the illusion of duality, separation, and disunity [asked to have legs broken and bodies removed]. [32.] As long as we remain in an egocentric cubbyhole of awareness defined by its rigid materialistic parameters [soldiers], we will interrupt the flow of potent, divine energies [break the legs] and prevent them from Christizing our intuitive and conceptual thought systems [the two men crucified with Jesus]. [33.] When we understand there is no duality [they did not break his legs], it will be because our Christ potential has been fully actualized into our Christhood [Jesus was already dead].

[34.] Once we have become fully Christed, even the most penetrating of materialistic thoughts [soldier's spear piercing Jesus' side] is transfused by the power of high potency universal love (heart center). Because of its perfect and sacred energetics, our newly acquired Christ Consciousness immediately transforms any residue of sense consciousness into its higher spiritual equivalent. This spontaneous at-one-ment (etherized blood) and chimeric purification (vitalized water) lay the foundation for our newly Christed consciousness and the consciousness of humankind to once again transcend physicality and become pure Spirit.

---

[b] *Our 'calling' represents our decision to incarnate into human form. It is based on the error belief that we are separated from Spirit. To master our 'calling' means we must, once and for all, move beyond our attachment for 'skin school' experiences.*

35. At this level of illumination we live, move, and have our being as Conscious spiritual beings [the man who testified]. 36. It is the journey from sense consciousness to Christ Consciousness [scripture being fulfilled] that completes our conscious unification (no bones broken) with Spirit. The story of our soul reformation [scripture] is a *re-covery* from our *sacred wounds*[c] or *soul piercings* (the incarnations we have endured on our journey toward enlightenment). 37. These 'wounds' could also be referred to as *sacred piercings* (our souls being thrust into matter) which provide "skin school" experiences for us to matriculate through the self-imposed illusion of our separation from Spirit.

The Quiet Roar of Enlightenment

38. Despite our newly acquired state of illumination [our Joseph of Arimatheaness], there may still be a residue of earthy thoughts [our Jewishness] which remind us of our pre-Christed level of awareness [the body of Jesus]. This last vestige of willful earthiness [the Pilate of us] clings to the possibility of a return [permission to take the body] to our pre-illumined state of consciousness. 39. However, because we are illumined, our intellectual understanding of our spiritual nature [the enlightened Nicodemus of us], which grew out of the initial unawareness [came to Jesus at night] of our divine heirship, has blossomed immeasurably. We know the truth about the eternality of Spirit [mixture of myrrh and aloes] in the context of our completed soul work [75 pounds[d] or 7+5=12, which symbolizes spiritual wholeness, completion].

40. In this increasingly vivified state of illumination and superior intellectual understanding [the two men], we are truly able to transcend the limitations of our physicality [wrap

---

[c] *The sacred wounds (pierced hands, feet, and side) represent our five physical senses which must become Christized.*

[d] *Some references say 100 pounds, which also represents spiritual wholeness.*

body with linen]. ⁴¹· We prepare ourselves to enter the exalted gateway into a higher, more blissful and virginal state of consciousness [Arimathea's unused garden tomb]. ⁴²· We have moved from a pre-Christed state of awareness [the Day of Preparation] into a Christed state of being, which knows only wholeness and perfection. Our 'entombment' represents the *quiet roar* of enlightenment where vital energies raise every fiber of our being to its monistic wholeness.

Chapter Twenty

The Theodynamics of Our Resurrection Potential

¹· At the moment we become aware of our complete and absolute union with Spirit [the first day of the week],[a] we realize we have separated ourselves from the gravitational pull of a materiality-focused perspective [darkness]. Our devotion to the Truth [the Mary Magdalene of us] has taken us to the 'gateway of higher consciousness' [came to the tomb], which means we have moved beyond the illusion of separation and duality [the stone was removed from the entrance]. ²· It is our unfailing devotion to the Truth [the Mary Magdalene of us], fortified by our uncompromised faithfulness [the Simon Peter of us] and universality of love [our John quality], which recognizes that our Christ potential [the Lord Jesus of us] has become fully actualized [taken from the tomb]. Since we have not reached this state of Christed awareness before, we cannot comprehend its quantum implications [do not know where they have laid him/put him].

³· If we discipline ourselves to remain at this high state of awareness [the tomb], our universality of love [our John quality] and mature faith [the Simon Peter of us] will become even more potent. ⁴· It is our univer-

---

[a] *Transforming potential into actuality, or thoughts into things, is a seven step (day) process (initiation): initial awareness, insight, imagination, resolve, wisdom, love, and stillness.*

sal love quality [the John of us (our interior harmonizing agent)] which prepares the way [outruns the other] for our mature faith [our Peter quality (our internal knowing instrument)] to *ray forth* its cosmic clarity [the empty tomb]. [5.] In the early stages of our Christed journey, we are fully aware that we have subordinated our ego [bent over] by elevating our understanding of truth principles [strips of linen] to the degree that what were once revolutionary spiritual insights are inadequate [did not go in] for the potent vibrational work we are preparing to do. [6.] However, at this level of heightened awareness [go into the tomb] our faith center [the Simon Peter of us] is fully aligned with its cosmic expression. We know intuitively that our rudimentary understanding of basic truth principles [strips of line/linen wrappings] [7.] has grown to a more pansophic level [burial cloth around Jesus' head]. This level of monistic understanding [cloth folded up separate from linen] is far superior to our rudimentary spiritual development.

[8.] Because our faith center is so strong at this level of Christed awareness [our John capacity], it permeates every aspect of our being [He saw and believed]. [9.] Even though we have a well-developed inner knowing (faith) and a superior harmonic aptitude (love), we are still neophytes at the Christed level of consciousness. We find it difficult to understand that the genealogy of our spiritual unfoldment [scripture] has its origins in the truth that our Christ potential [the Jesus of us] can become actualized [must rise] in an ego-driven consciousness [the dead] which makes it a practice to deny our innate divinity.

Our Devotion to the Truth Electrifies Us

[10.] With our inner harmonics (love) and interior knowing (faith) so well-developed [went back to homes], [11.] our highly sensitive [weeping] and evolved psychic ability [Mary (Magdalene)] helps us gain the clarity we need to see beyond [stood outside the empty tomb] the initial glimpse into our new world of awakening. 12. In this heightened state of illumination, our psychically-sharpened intellect and highly spiritualized intuition [angels in white seated at the hand and foot locations] characterize our initial unfoldment experience.

13. Because of this attenuated receptivity, our sensitivity [weeping] toward experiencing a major shift in consciousness from Christed potential [my Lord (the Jesus of us)] to realized Christhood is a little disconcerting. 14. However, the moment of transition is usually so smooth that we fail to recognize we have gone from one *cusp of consciousness* to another [do not recognize Jesus].

15. As mentioned previously, our super-charged sensitivity (the Magdalene effect) is the out-picturing of a lower vibrational form of psychic awareness which we try to adjust to its higher, more super-conscious vibration [tell me where you have laid him].

16. There will come a point, shortly after the actualization of our Christhood, when we become absolutely clear [Jesus calls to Mary] that we are the product of the highest possible spiritual Source [Rabboni/Teacher].

17. Just as we have learned at each pre-Christed level of awareness, we must be willing to release current knowledge to expand our capacity for greater knowledge. Once we are Christed, the same truth holds ["Do not touch me/hold onto me]. As we grow in our Christness, we will transform our subconscious and conscious *selves* [brothers] so that they, too, become *indivisibly* linked [return/ascend] with the One Reality [Father/God], as did Jesus (the Nazarene).

18. Although we are neophytes at the fully Christed level of awareness, our devotion to the Truth [the Mary Magdalene

of us] electrifies our higher spiritual qualities [disciples] with its transformative powers [I have seen the Lord].

Over-Coming the Staining Effects of Error

19. Because our Christed awareness is a newly-acquired awareness, the height [evening] of our understanding [day] depends on the maturation of our spiritual qualities [disciples]. We may not be fully confident in our ability to deny [lock the doors] the power of outer appearances and the encrusted religious perspectives [our Jewishness] that come with them. However, we need only remind ourselves that we have actualized our Christ potential [the Jesus of us] and can find the harmony, balance, and equilibrium [peace] we seek by going into the Silence [be still]. 20. As we contemplate our progress, we will see that the staining effects of error, even the most chronically ingrained materialistic thoughts (errors which lead to *sacred wounds*) cannot find residence [the disciples were overjoyed] in our current state of consciousness.

21. We must not hesitate to affirm the inner harmony and balance [peace] that 'practicing the presence' (being still) can give us. We must remember what our spiritual resume looks like: the same Christ (the formative expression of God the [Father]) that expressed Itself as Jesus is expressing Itself *as* us. 22. When we realize that truth without any equivocation [he breathed on them], we will feel the surge of the highly-charged vital energies of the inner fire [the Holy Spirit][b] electrifying our consciousness, launching us toward the Soul work ahead.

23. Once we have erased error thoughts and replaced them with a consciousness grounded in Truth [forgiveness], they are dissolved. On the other hand, if we fail to purge our consciousness of error [do not forgive] we will continue to struggle with the

---
[b] *See Chapter 14:16, 21*

illusions propagated by outer appearances [will not be forgiven].

Turning a Petulant Intellect Into Cosmic Intelligence

24. What is described above is all part of the transformation process. Our newly-acquired cosmic (quantum) understanding [the Thomas/Didymus of us] is still a newly acquired understanding. But it is an essential quality for our soul work along with the other highly-charged spiritual qualities [the twelve]. Even at this level of a quantumly sensitized awareness, our ability to comprehend higher spiritual truths unfolds more slowly than other highly-spiritualized qualities [(Thomas) was absent].

25. The dynamic tension between our fully quickened inner qualities [the 'other disciples'] and our evolved, but petulant intellect (the Thomas of us) will clearly become evident throughout this phase of our enlightenment. The source of this internal tension stems from the intellect's attachment to our pre-Christed struggle with the incarnational implications (the *sacred wounds*) associated with the somatic fruits of the belief in duality and separation.

26. In order to fully understand the dynamic process [a week later][c] of going from Spirit into matter and from matter back to Spirit (from potential to actuality, and from the manifest to the unmanifest), we must harmonize all of our spiritual qualities [the disciples, including Thomas]. When we have completely eliminated [locked the doors] error thoughts from our consciousness [house], our receptivity to our newly- attained Christness [Jesus entered] will always bring us inner harmony and balance [peace] because we are *The Presence* vibrating (being still) *as* us.

27. It is the incarnational 'story' itself (the *sacred wounds*) which the intellect clings to as it seeks the clarity it needs to comprehend our innate spirituality. As

---
[c] *See footnote 'a' in this chapter.*

has been mentioned before (verse 24), the intellect, even at this stage in its quickening, unfolds at a slower pace than other Christed qualities.

28. Nevertheless, we will be able to turn intellectual knowledge into spiritual understanding and recognize our Christ potential [Lord] for what It is – God (the One Reality, the Absolute) in latency at the point of us.

29. It is in the nature of our initial unfoldment for us, regardless of our degree of illumination, to want proofs of the efficacy of higher truths. Eventually, we will witness a transformation of our thought system, which shows a more intuitional intellect, one which follows the lead of our heart center by surrendering to its Christed capacities.

30. We must understand that at this level of Christed awareness (our Jesus Christness) many higher, but unknown spiritual truths [miracles] lie dormant [are not recorded] in our lifelong journey [book] toward rediscovering the full implications of our innate divinity. 31. In each of our incarnations [these are written] we have opportunities to discover that the same Christ that expressed Itself as Jesus' true Spiritual Self in human form [the Son of God] is the same Christ that expresses Itself *as* us. It is our chief incarnational task to have the courage, discernment, and faith to claim [believe] that truth.

Chapter Twenty-One

Achieving Complete Harmony With the Trinity of Trinities

1. Once we move beyond the illusion of duality and separation and see consciousness as the ground of all being [a Sea of Tiberius perspective], we have reached that exalted state of cosmic awareness [the Jesus Christ of us] which defines our new

2. The spiritual qualities which are particularly helpful at this juncture in our enlightenment are unequivocable faith [the Simon Peter of us], cosmic intelligence [the Thomas of us], and total openness and receptivity to cosmic truths [our Nathanael quality]. These three qualities would have remained under-expressed by us at a lower vibration [our Cana capacity]. Other highly-charged spiritual qualities are also present, such as a high degree of inviolate wisdom [our James, son of Zebedee quality]; love raised to its universal resonance [our John, son of Zebedee quality]; enthusiastic, but controlled zealousness [our Simon the Zealot quality]; and illumined imagination [the Bartholomew of us] that keep us energized and expectant as we explore our expanded thought universe.

3. As we explore the limitlessness of our super-heated awareness, it is important to remember that even though we are operating at a super-conscious level with enhanced spiritual abilities, we must not allow our inviolate faith [the Simon Peter of us] to slip back into impetuous faith. Seeking divine ideas [fish] at a fully-Christed level of awareness means honoring our Christ Connection. It means affirming our good from the awareness of our oneness with the Eternal Isness (the One Reality, the Infinite Indivisibleness), as we advance through each plane[a] of consciousness. If we neglect to do that, we will find that putting our ego first on any plane of being limits our continued spiritual growth [they caught no fish].

4. Depending solely on our incarnational 'resumes' [the disciples did not recognize Jesus] as we become acclimated at each *cusp of consciousness* [early in the morning] keeps the vital energies of our Christ Self dormant [Jesus stood on the shore].

---

[a] *There are many planes of awareness. As we matriculate through each plane (dimension of cosmic awareness) we need to remember that we are the Christ expressing Itself as us no matter how many dimensions of being [schools] we choose to experience.*

5. Without that conscious Christ Connection, we lose opportunities to receive divine ideas [fish]. 6. As in our previous states of awareness, if our consciousness [net] is Truth-centered [throw nets on the right] our ability to remain in the world but not of the world [boat] will provide opportunities to receive many divine ideas [a large catch of fish], ideas which will help us master the art of living on any plane of being.

7. When our love [our Johnness] for the Truth, and faith [the Simon Peter of us] in the enduring presence of our Christ Self are rightly adjusted, we express our Christness [wrap the outer garment (knowledge of our *indivisibility* with Spirit) around him] instead of repressing it [for he had taken it off]. From that Christed demeanor, we can handle any incarnational challenge [jump into water].

8. If we allow our illumined spiritual qualities [disciples] to express themselves, we will maintain a positive and enlightened perspective [follow in the boat], one which has a wholesome [100 yards/90 meters] thought environment teeming with divine ideas [a net full of fish]. 9. In such a purified mental environment [fire of burning coals], the number of divine ideas [fish] which surface will only be limited by our ability to tap into Universal Substance [bread]. 10. It is important to remember to lift those divine ideas [fish] from the perspective of our Christ Consciousness [the fully illumined Jesus of us]. 11. With our faith [our Simon Peter quality] centered in our Christness, we can keep a positive outlook [climb aboard the boat] by being grounded in Spirit [dragged the net ashore]. From that elevated perspective, our entire thought universe [the net is full of fish] is in complete harmony with the Trinity of Trinities [represented by the number 153 modified to $9(1+5+3=9)$].[b] Our super-conscious awareness [net] is limitless in its capacity to comprehend the Infinite (the One Reality, the Eternal Isness, Divine Mind) because

---

[b] *Trinity of Trinities:* God, Son, Holy Spirit; Mind, Idea, Expression; body, mind, soul.

we have moved beyond any notion of duality and separation [the net is not torn].

12. Because our awareness is at such a heightened *pitch* (we, like the Christ as Jesus, will have attained Christ Consciousness) we will be able to comprehend (eat) quantum (cosmic) truths without any equivocation or reservation [they knew it was the Lord].

13 From this Christed orientation [the Jesus Christ of us], we can draw divinely-inspired ideas [fish] from Universal Supply [bread] at will. 14. On whatever plane of consciousness we are operating (physical, astral, ethereal, etc.), we can divinely order (symbolized by the number three) our good by using our highly-charged spiritual capacities [disciples] to master our temporal experiences.

Out-Growing an Immature Faith and In-Growing a Full Throttle One

15. We must pay attention to the quality of our *thoughts, words,* and *actions*[c] if we expect to strengthen our Truth walks on any plane of existence. It is our unequivocal receptivity to Truth from an impeccably strong faith center [the Simon Peter of us] that helps us see that divine ideas come from a Christed consciousness [Do you love me more than these?]. This level of heightened discernment comes from a mature love for the Truth [our John-ness]. Because we are at such an illuminated level of enlightenment, we must make it a practice to Christize [feed] all of our *thoughts* [lambs].

16. We must become adept at trusting our inner knowing [the Simon Peter of us], and unhesitatingly ground it in the love for Truth [our John capacity] so we have no difficulty Christizing [feeding] all of our *words* [sheep].

17. At the risk of being redundant, we must become so unfailingly trusting in our inner guidance [the Simon Peter of us] and in our being able to consistently harmonize all of our thoughts and words that we are

---
[c] *These three qualities can also refer to body, mind, and soul; Mind, Idea, Expression; subconscious, conscious, and superconscious; physical, mental, emotional.*

able to Christize [feed] all of our *actions* [sheep] as well.

[18.] When we are neophytes [younger] in our spiritual development we tend to have an impetuous, blind, wistful sort of faith [went where we wanted] which springs from our own limited understanding (we dress ourselves) of the dynamic properties of faith. However, as we mature [are old] in our faith we realize [stretch out our hands] that we must trust the guidance of our Christ Self instead of an unenlightened egocentric personality [someone else] which has its own sense-soaked agenda [will dress you]. Following it will compromise our spiritual growth [lead us where we do not want to go]. [19.] We must remind ourselves that we must outgrow (die to) an impetuous, whimsical, immature faith and transform it [glorify] into a dynamic inner quality that is the rock of our spiritual growth.

The Quantum Legacy of Our Incarnational 'Stories'

[20.] Faith [the Peter of us] is always underwritten by our persistent and consistent love for the Truth [the John of us]. It is our love for the Truth which fortifies our Christed perspective [leans on Jesus] and keeps us aligned with our Higher Self. Our uncompromised love for the Truth will keep us from mis-stepping [betraying], so we remain devoted to our spiritual growth. [21.] The strength of our faith [our Peterness] depends on the depth of inner knowing and confidence we bring to any life experience, regardless of which plane of consciousness we find ourselves. On the other hand, the great harmonizing capacity within us [Universal Love] is not only cumulative but foundational. We do not have to question its eternal validity or reliability.

[22.] Unlike our sense-dependent intellectual knowing which must re-acclimate itself as we go from one *cusp of consciousness* to another, our harmonizing capacity (our heart-centered, intuitional understanding) has a built-in integrative *switch,* which allows us to sense our unity [remain alive] with all that is at each plane of being until we can grasp the nature of our Christness [until I return] at that level of being. Essentially, we are love personified, while faith is something we acquire in various degrees depending on our level of expanded awareness.

23. Having said that, there is a primordial energy current[d] [rumor] within us that super-charges our wisdom (the James of us) and love (the John of us) faculties [brothers], creating a harmonic convergence which suggests that we will always remain [will not die] at a Christed level of consciousness. Because our Universal Love quality is essentially pre-wired as a unifying influence [to remain alive] at each level of our evolving awareness, it naturally follows that we have a perennial capacity to sense our Christness [the return] at each plane of being.

24. It is our incarnational responsibility – and privilege -- to harmonize, integrate, and unify (testify) all aspects of our being so that we can fully actualize and then demonstrate our Christhood. As we harmonize body, mind, and soul in each plane of being [write them down], we will find it is necessary to underwrite all of our soul work with the love that passes all *mis*understanding.

25. As mentioned previously, we will have many opportunities (lifetimes), as did Jesus (of Nazareth), to actualize and fully express our Christhood. The important thing to remember is that we must focus on our present incarnational experience.

Although we have access to our previous incarnations (books) through many helpful modalities[e] [if every one of them were written down], these 'stories' are tucked away in our Quantum Self[f] because our waking conscious-

---
[d] *See John:3:14; 14:16,21; 15:26; 16:7; 20:22.*
[e] *Dreams, intuitions, past life regressions, hypnosis, meditation, astral-kinesis, etc.*
[f] *The multi-incarnational composite of all of our past and concurrent intra-dimensional states of being, including our present 'skin school' experience, which will also be integrated when we make our transition.*

ness [the whole world] would not be able to sustain such a multidimensional overload. One day we will outgrow our fixation for duality and separation, and affirm our oneness with Spirit. In the meantime, in whatever dimension of being we find ourselves, we must strive to be the best Christs we can be.

Bil Holton, Ph.D. currently shares spiritual leadership responsibilities with his wife, Cher, in the growing Unity Spiritual Life Center they co-minister in Durham, North Carolina. He is a Licensed Unity Minister, and has been affiliated with the Unity spiritual education movement for thirty years. As a student of metaphysics for over twenty years, Dr. Holton believes Biblical scripture has a deeper spiritual meaning, which enriches the literal text and elevates it beyond its dogmatic and parochial limitations.

His spiritual mission is to lead, guide, and inspire people all over the world to live faithfully, lovingly, and wisely at the speed of their Christ Consciousness. While he has authored and co-authored over twenty-five books with Cher, Bil believes his metaphysical translations of the Gospels are his most fulfilling works to date.

On a personal note, the Holtons like to push the envelope and maintain their zest for life by taking what they call "Indiana Jones Adventures," such as white-water rafting, sky diving, and fire walking. American-style ballroom dancing is also in their DNA. Although they have retired their competitive dance shoes, Bil and Cher love to perform ballroom showcases and exhibitions. Their two sons, beautiful daughters-in-law, and three incredible grandchildren, all live nearby. Their visits are always joyful.

Other spiritually-oriented books by Rev. Dr. Bil Holton:

The Gospel of Matthew, New Metaphysical Version
The Gospel of Mark, New Metaphysical Version
The Gospel of Luke, New Metaphysical Version
*Crackerjack Choices: 200 of the Best Choices You Will Ever Make**
*Right Thoughts, Right Choices, Right Actions: 200 of the Best Choices Unity People Will Ever Make**
*Business Prayers for Millenium Managers**
*Get Over It! The Truth About What You Know That Just Ain't So***
*Get Over These, Too! More Truth About What You Know That Just Ain't So!***

*Co-authored with Rev. Dr. Cher Holton
**Co-authored with Rev. Dr. Paul Hasselbeck

To order copies of Dr. Holton's books, and request information about scheduling him for speaking engagements, visit his website at http://www.metaphysicalbible.net or call his office at 877.819.7489.

You may contribute to the New Metaphysical Version Project, which supports Dr. Holton's work, by visiting the official website, http://www.metaphysicalbible.net or by contacting Dr. Holton at his toll-free office number, 877.819.7489.